Re-Inventing
DENTISTRY

A new vision for building and marketing your dental practice

Dr. Rinesh Ganatra

ISBN: 1466211903
ISBN 13: 9781466211902

Library of Congress Control Number: 2011914172
CreateSpace, North Charleston, SC

DEDICATED to my parents, Ramesh and Uma Ganatra, without their love and support of who I am and what I do I would have never learned the things I did.

CONTENTS

INTRODUCTION
Recreate Everything

What if your patients walked into your office and were astonished by the design of your office and the friendliness, professionalism, and expertise of your staff? What if they told you your office felt different than any other health care practice they had ever been to? You ignited their interest because, unlike most dentists who still use traditional advertisements for their services, you were the expert in their area, and they had already seen you. No, not on TV. They watched online videos that you created, videos about dental health and lifestyle choices that inform, entertain, and sell your expertise. Your enthusiasm is so contagious, why wouldn't they want to come see you? And, what if, when they walked into your office, everything they had seen and heard of you was confirmed, and it elevated their comfort level as if they've always known you? Imagine your patients commenting that yours is the best dental office that they had ever stepped into. What if they loved and appreciated your staff and told you that just seeing them lifted their spirits and made them *feel* great about their day? Better yet, what if they expressed to you that your team is exceptional because they are an extension of you, the owner? How would that make you feel? What I'm describing is an experience you wouldn't have in a typical dentist's office, but it can be. My challenge to you is to stop *what* you're doing and *how* you're doing it, and hit *refresh*. You can, and in doing so, you would be re-inventing dentistry. Imagine that!

I wrote this book to help you create exactly that—to give you the systems and *success setup* to create this atmosphere in your office wherever you may be practicing right now. Whether you've been in practice for twenty years or two months, every dentist aspires to something bigger, something greater, and all dentists want to be a positive, motivational influence on their patients. Don't you want to raise your standard for service and presentation? Even if you've just graduated and are fresh out of dental school, the dream that you harbored throughout your years in dental school inspired you to push on, to reach that place where you can create dentistry your way, the way you always felt it should be. Even if you already have a practice and know *how it all works* in dentistry, you're probably looking for more inspiration to fuel your day, to realize that vision that's stirring in your mind somewhere. I wrote this book to re-ignite that deep desire slumbering in all of us, the desire to practice *your* way using the tools available to us today so that you can re-invent dentistry the way you've always *felt* it should be.

Most dentists don't realize that the possibilities are endless and have no clue as to what can be done with their offices today when they utilize the powerful tools and techniques that are available to all of us. In this book, I will show you how to put it all together: how to build your office from the ground up and how to market your services and grow your business to create a tribe of raving fans that return and refer. If you want to know how to design the next recall postcard, this is not the book for you. But if you want to utilize the psychology of connecting with your patients through your online presence, videos, social media culture, and a website that answers their questions before they even meet you, then read on. *As you will soon realize, it all has to come full circle; your message must complete itself when your patients come into your office. But live beyond yourself when they leave as well.* Unless you complete the picture with a phenomenal office setup, you can't paint that crystal-clear vision of excellence for your patients when they walk in the door. This book will tie it all together. Impact, influence, and income are the goals of every practice owner.

So, if you currently own an office, then take advantage of the points and systems that I present. If you are thinking of buying an office or becoming an owner, then use the strategies and structures that I illustrate during your transition. If you want to have a more appealing office, dig into the important elements of design that I cover. If you are currently running a successful practice, then discover how you can integrate the systems that I have laid out. If you want to know how to enhance your online presence, master the art of social media, or harness social proof at its finest. Then, you must read about the Online Presence Triangle. Last, if you are a new graduate who survived those four grueling years of dental school, then make this book your vision board for your new practice. I only wish that someone had shared this framework with me when I began my journey. Knowing these systems will place you in a new paradigm of dentists! Come and join me there—on top.

WHY ME?

When I graduated from dental school in 2002, I worked at five different offices and hated them all. Phew! What I experienced was different from what I learned in dental school. Most of these offices didn't even have light handle covers; they overdiagnosed their patients; and they under-communicated, all at the same time! I thought to myself, *Gee what the heck are these places thinking to be practicing in this fashion?* Under these circumstances, how could they expect that patients would look forward to seeing them? Is this really an acceptable standard in dentistry? Patients came in and waited for hours for treatment and, oftentimes, they would leave dissatisfied with the care they received. That feeling of empty trust led them to the office of the next dentist down the street. Every day this would happen, and it soon became the standard for dentistry in that region. This was certainly not my vision. So, I made a commitment to myself to move away from that situation and create something better for both me and my patients.

So, in this despair, I began my journey. In four short years I built three successful, state-of-the-art offices in Orange County, California, saturated with hundreds of dentists who were there before I entered the community. *For those four to five years I was fully immersed in creating, building, and launching three businesses without a single patient scheduled to see me before I opened.*

Within the first three years, the first office was valued at a little under $900,000! We tripled the growth from the first year to the third. Wouldn't it be useful to see how I tripled growth in three years in a building with three other dentists, all of whom competed for the same community of patients? Even more important, I created a thriving dental brand in south Orange County that continues to prosper today.

This book is a result of my creating a framework of success from what I learned based on the obstacles I overcame and insights that were attained in starting three businesses from scratch and growing them to thousands of patients in a very short span of time. It is all here, packaged up into success systems, techniques, and tools from which you can re-*invent dentistry, no matter where you are in your dental career.* **Yes, this *is* powerful information, but more so, it is a matter of a *unique perspective* that has helped me launch all three offices to success.**

In the first part of the book, I discuss how to build your office from the ground up. Everything from finding a location, designing it, hiring a contractor, to the construction process itself. The second part of the book, shows you how to create winning systems inside your practice by focusing on *attracting patients, treatment planning,* and getting patients to *return* to you. You will learn what's critical for creating your dream team, mastering the front office phones, and integrating effective treatment planning skills into your practice. In the third part of the book, I review the Online Presence Triangle® to enhance the power of your email, your website, video, and social media. Using this online framework you'll be ready to market your new or current office and bring in a steady flow of patients each month. In doing so, you will increase your presence and reach in your community. With this knowledge you will be ready and armed with what it takes to create, run, and market your practice today.

TRUST AND TRANSPARENCY

There is something new and exciting going on in our world today, and it involves *trust* and *transparency*. Dentistry is intimately connected to this paradigm shift in consumer consciousness in health care. *Social media and, more importantly, social proof are directly linked to the mind-set that fuels trust and transparency.* This *shift* is affecting the health care marketplace and will affect you as a dentist and how your patients choose you, interact with you, and maintain a relationship with you and your office staff. *Consumers and patients across the developing world are now selecting what they want from you before they even meet you.* Understand what I am saying here. They are selecting services from you before they even see you or even experience you or your team. The top two aspects making this change possible is your patients' need for *trust and transparency.* With the collapse of the financial markets in 2008 and our recent plunge into recessionary-type spending habits, our patients now need trust and transparency more than ever before to accelerate their buying decisions. As dentists, we are not immune to this type of evaluation from our patients. This new world in how we exchange monetary value for services will change the business of dentistry forever. Let's begin this journey of change together and create a newfound success in this exciting time!

Within this book are the proven systems and secrets to building, marketing, and growing your office to an endless potential. You will learn exactly what it takes to build, grow, and market your office in this new day of dentistry using the online technologies that are so readily available to us. You will learn what to do to bring patients *to you*, create an effective treatment plan for them, and have them return and refer back to you!

What better way to focus on all the important elements than by recreating them from scratch. *When you create something from the ground up, you have total control of how you manufacture the end result.* These systems, techniques, and key points can be superimposed on any dental practice situation you may be involved in, whether it means building your dream office or enhancing your current one.

Chapter 1

WHY BUILD AN OFFICE?

*We are all creators with the need to express our dreams
through the way we live our life and how we work.*

There are so many dental offices out there. When I first got out of school in 2002, I worked at five different offices and, to be quite honest, I hated all of them with the exception of one. If you are like most new dentists who just graduated within the last three years, then you know that our field is really different than any other field out there. On the flip side, if you have been practicing for quite some time and even own your own office, you understand through experience that there are some distinctively unique elements in our profession. **Here are just a few of them:**

No other field requires you to go to school for eight to ten years and then work with individuals who may only have a high school diploma and maybe a couple years of college. This creates such a polarity in your team. Dental school doesn't prepare you for this challenge, nor does it teach you how to manage your staff and increase revenue.

After graduating from that much schooling, most people work in nice buildings with accommodations for personal items, maybe even company lounges, staff relaxation rooms, cafeterias, and overall impressive-looking environments. For dentists, this couldn't be farther from the truth. Dental offices, in general, are really a hole in the wall at many locations. Sometimes the original owner has been there for decades and has not upgraded the equipment, furniture, or even bothered with the decor. It is important to know that most of these offices consist of a solo practitioner, or they are a mom-and-pop type business with the mind-set and philosophy of the owner built into the presence of the office. *In essence, the office is only as strong as the owner's weakest attributes.*

The marketing strategies of the office are really a personal compilation of what the owner thinks works and, if you are an associate, your input is challenged by the years and even decades of *doing things "the way it's been done in the past."*

ASK YOURSELF SOME IMPORTANT QUESTIONS:

How can you break through the innate challenges that hold true in our field when you step into to the real world?

How can you initiate a performance shift in the way you practice so you can harness the new paradigm shift in health care?

If you own your own office, what are its weakest points, and which one of those could you change in just a few days to yield the highest lifestyle and financial return?

In order to gain insight from these questions, you must know the biggest factor that influences all of the answers.

First, ask yourself what you want out of your career and how you want to practice dentistry. What's your vision for yourself? Without clarity, there is no power, no influence and, ultimately, no direction. Take a moment to answer these questions:

- What is your vision?
- What kind of office do you want to have?
- What do you want your office to say about you and your staff?
- What do you want your office to say to your patients?
- Most importantly, what kind of impression do you want to leave on your patients?
- Are you motivated by the thought of moving into someone else's spot or business and paying for their junk?
- Can your vision be superimposed on what existed prior to your arrival?

If you really want to live life on your terms and carry forward the vision that you have for yourself, then it is crucial that you give yourself the knowledge-base and information you need to realize your dreams and plan your reality.

You won't find anything more rewarding than creating the office of your dreams, an office that represents you and your vision for how you want to practice dentistry and treat your patients.

The insights and information that I share with you in the following pages will teach you the most accurate and comprehensive way to achieve this dream.

You see, when you buy an existing practice you really are buying someone else's junk, a worn-out copy of someone else's played-out record with numerous scratches, misinterpretations, and lost potential. Not only that, but you will also be paying big money for an old, worn-out blueprint.

Let me give you an example here. Let's say that Dr. Old Office is making one million a year in gross income in his office that has been there for twenty years. In the course of his time there, he has treated over 10,000 patients. In California, practices can be valued at about 85–100 percent of gross income. So, in this situation, you will likely pay anywhere from $850,000 to one million dollars for this office. If you use a well-known dental financier who will give you close to 100 percent financing for your office, then you will owe the bank roughly $9,000–$11,000 a month for about seven years. When you take over the seller's office, do you think all of those patients are going to stay with the office once they figure out that *their* dentist, who has been there for twenty years, is leaving? The answer is *no*! You paid for all this, though. It's important to realize that as soon as you purchase this office, by the virtue of the purchase, you have lost some money on it. So, from day one, your "asset" has devalued. Let's think about this: can you take a one million dollar dental office to two million in five years? It's possible but very unlikely, and even more challenging than getting it to one million.

Now, let's flip the coin here. Can you take a $250,000 office to $800,000 in five years? Or, if you're really pushing for the gold, can you take that same office to one million in gross revenues in five to seven years? Yes, you can, if you know how to grow a business. Growth from the ground up is very predictable as long as you follow a proven formula. BUT growing something close to its saturation point can be very challenging. In the $250,000 office scenario, you can make 200–400 percent on your investment. You can start your office for $250,000 and sell it for $800,000–$1,000.000 and leave some money on the table for the next person to take it to 1.5 million or 2 million. You could accomplish this with the direction of *your* vision in *your* environment. So, build it for $250,000 and then sell it for one million! Not a bad return on your investment within five years or so.

Now, you might be thinking that it's not your goal or desire to just sell your office. Well, that's fine, too, as you can still practice in it and keep growing it so that one day you will sell it at an even higher valuation. When going into business, you must plan for and know your final destination, and a part of that destination is the selling of that business. You must always look at your business from the reference point of its worth at the time of selling. This is the true value or sweat equity of your business.

As you can see, there is tremendous financial potential in building your office from scratch.

Chapter 2

LOCATION =
ENVIRONMENT

Where you are is not an indication of where you will go,
but it sure is nice to be in a cool place.

Location is the starting point. We have all heard the phrase, "Location, location, location," the overused mantra emphasizing the importance of selecting a great location for your business. As dentists, what does location mean to us? Is it on a cliff overlooking the ocean? Although this may be the ideal location for a dream home, it's not necessarily a great place to build practice. Say, for example, there is a ton of traffic on one street that leads to that cliff overlooking the ocean. It's likely that this road is congested with tourists who are there for a short-term visit on vacation. I would love to have an office overlooking the ocean and think this would be ultra cool, but this is not the most practical location. When you look for a location to build or even purchase an office, get to know the surrounding areas and environment first.

Remember that location describes an area on a map, but the environment actually personifies that area. A good location is one that is situated in a great local environment that gives it its unique personality. Dentistry is a local business, and most of your patients will travel within a twenty-mile radius. Understanding the psychology and grasping the caliber of this twenty-mile radius is an important part of your research when building your office. Yes, you will have those patients who will arrive at your practice after driving for an hour but, for the most part, the majority of your patients will have driven around twenty miles for their visit. For instance, many would think a busy street would provide a good environment. This may hold true for some regions, but even better would be a busy, foot-traffic area well-situated near a shopping or medical plaza. This is so because foot traffic is actually more interactive than busy street traffic. It gives a more personal feel in a high-volume environment.

Using online tools, such as Zipskinny.com and Zillow.com, you can see what your local environment looks like using your zip code. Zillow helps you to evaluate local home prices in the area. For instance, if you notice an overwhelming number of foreclosures in that area, starting a practice there might not be a good idea. Areas like that, where people are actually moving out of that local environment, should be avoided when starting a business. There are countless online tools that can give you free demographical data. For example, you can see what the average household income is in your area, age group, male versus female population, education level, and even marital status. Do you think that knowing your local market would be helpful in selecting how to market to them? Isn't marketing to a primarily younger population different from marketing to those over sixty-five? Such knowledge gives you the power to design more effective marketing pieces; it also gives you the edge while you figure out how you can add more value to that specific population. A primarily geriatric population, for example, may want to replace their old, uncomfortable dentures with implants or even implant retained overdentures. Instead of veneers, maybe they want better fitting, removable prostheses.

When I built my first office in Rancho Santa Margarita, California, in 2005, *Money* magazine had named it "One of the Best Places to Live in the Western United States" a few years prior. Now, don't get me wrong here; it's not like Maui or Newport Beach, both of which boast extravagant ocean-front communities and beach homes. More so, it was evaluated on the basis of local schools, the resources available for new families and their children, community parks, nearby restaurants, and a reasonable valuation for home prices. The median average income was $65,000–$70,000.

After researching your zip code, you must consider two other factors. This is especially true if you are *building your office* and will draw from your community to create a consistent flow of patients. When selecting a location to build your office, evaluate its *value* based on these two critical points:

1. **What is the *regional* environment like?** For example, are you located in a big city, a suburb, or a small town? Your points of focus within your community will change depending on your regional environment. Here are some categories of regional environment you should be familiar with. Keep these categories in mind when creating a plan to integrate your office within the community:

   - **Schools** signify strength in a community. Schools show that families are living nearby and that they are looking for family-related services near their home, such as dentistry. Schools nearby also tells us that there are teachers, some of whom may have excellent dental insurance, who are looking for your services. Getting involved at the school (in health day, for example) provides an opportunity for you to get to know the teachers. Thus, networking in a close-knit community like this will get the word out about your practice.
   - **Water communities**, or beach communities, are known for their easy-going, laid back lifestyles.
   - **Union-related communities** have workers in unions who usually have excellent insurance benefits, which might cover most dental treatments without a maximum per year.
   - **Retirement communities** are excellent communities to be near as you will likely get a lot of patients with crown and bridge concerns and an interest in implant dentistry, overdentures, and other forms of removable prosthodontics.
   - **Corporate circles-** Large nearby corporations are an excellent source of new patients. Contacting their human resources team

and drafting up an agreement for their employees is a great way to gain more exposure within their company. Once a few individuals in a company come utilize your services they usually tell their co-workers, and before you know it they start sending more patients to you.

2. **What is the local environment like?** For example, is it in a cottage of other offices nestled behind large trees, or are there many retail shops within walking distance? The local environment affects the feel your patients have when they arrive at your office, before they even walk into your suite. The local environment also exposes specific demographics within your community. Here are the main traffic sources that you should keep in mind:

- **Retail traffic:** This traffic usually comes from two places: large anchor stores and small retail businesses. Anchor stores set the presence of a plaza. Large storefronts like Target, Home Depot, Kohl's, and Walmart each contribute something unique to the plaza. A plaza that has a Home Depot will have a different environment than, say, a Costco or a Walmart. Think outside of the box here as well, as an anchor store may even be a nice family restaurant that has heavy traffic for dinner and on weekends. It is important to note that sometimes your surrounding businesses set the tone for *your* business, even more so than the exterior of your office building. Small retail businesses, such as dry cleaners, donut shops, sporting goods stores, and gyms, have large volumes of people going in and out of those buildings. This is free visibility that I suggest you position your practice next to. All of these businesses produce a great deal of foot traffic, which is a free source of visibility that comes with proximity to other businesses.
- **Medical traffic:** If your practice is located near hospitals and medical buildings, you will see people coming and going into these types of businesses. Hospitals don't always bring significant visibility to a dental practice. With that being said, you could also talk to human resources within that hospital to bring in some of the doctors, nurses, and staff that work there.

- **Business traffic:** Business parks are those areas that contain the hustle and bustle of the work week but then quiet down on the weekends. One positive of business traffic is the opportunity to market your services to everyone in that business park and assure them that you will accommodate them during specific times of their work day.

HERE ARE SOME IDEAL LOCATIONS:

- **An office, medical, or retail plaza** near quality restaurants and small, high-traffic businesses, such as dry cleaners, clothing stores, and specialty food stores such as Trader Joe's, Whole Foods Market, and so on.
- **An office overlooking a busy street near a high-traffic plaza** gives you the best of both worlds. It is important to note that surrounding plazas must not be run-down or be in need of an extensive facelift. The third office that I built is located across from a large, California-based health food market called Mother's Market. It drew in a lot of health-conscious people and, since we had attractive building signage, people were familiar with our location.
- **An office in a robust business park** could work well for you. Depending on how well you market your services to this group of people, it can be a very lucrative location. For instance, you have thousands of prospective patients in those large high-rise buildings, but you must develop a plan to attract them. In this case, your office hours might vary since you'd be catering to professionals with rigid work schedules.
- **An office near a cluster of other medical and dental offices** on a busy street corner might be a great location. Granted, your office might not be distinguishable from other offices in this setting, but because the plaza has great signage for the different types of dental

practices in the area, it could work to your advantage. For instance, if you are an orthodontist or an endodontist surrounded by three general dentists, you can pull in a lot of your referrals from those nearby offices. Even though your office may not stand out from the others in the plaza, you still have visibility in the community since those living in the area will most likely know of the dentists and doctors in that cluster.

Although you may profit from the interdependence among dental practices in that plaza, you should be cognizant of the drawbacks. First, your office may not get any exposure at all since it is in a cottage-like cluster of other offices with ineffective signage. Second, in a new office build-out, noticeable signage and a strong presence are crucial for successful business.

SUITE LOCATIONS

Your suite location must be established early on. Where is your suite going to be located within your building? Are you next to the elevator? The pizza store? Being next door to a restaurant or pizza shop in the same plaza may cause some odor issues. Also, if your patients need to walk down a long hallway and pass three other dentists to get to your office, you could have a problem. Having the first suite in that long hallway would be the ideal situation. Get it? You also don't want your suite to look like it was the odd one out (by having it tucked in a dark corner at the end of the hall, for example).

6 BUILD-OUT POINTS FOR SUITE LOCATIONS

Listed below are the six build-out points you should look for when evaluating your suite location in the building that you are planning to construct your office within. If you are planning to buy an existing office, these same points would apply. All six of these build-out points are influenced by external, interior, or perimeter-type factors in relation to the suite.

1. **Windows in the suite** are the first thing I look for. Windows bring sunlight, and sunlight brings in energy. If your suite has windows, ensure that they are viewable windows. Viewable windows are window treatments that you can place your dental chairs in front of. Give the windows to the patients; don't keep them for the doctors' offices. We will go into this in more detail when I talk about suite design.

2. **Position of the suite** when you first walk in is a psychologically dominating area. If, when you first walk into a building you are on the floor where your office is located (first, second, or third floor), and your entry to your office is at the end of the hall or you must walk very far to get there, then this is not a dominant position within a floor. The dominant position is one where your office is seen in direct view upon arriving to the floor on which it is located. It subconsciously shows a position of authority on that floor and makes your presence priority.

3. **Structural posts** are tall steel posts that can be in your suite space. The significance of these is that they cannot be moved at any time as they are a fixed structural element in your suite that reinforces the building framework. The design of your suite is always limited by the location of these posts. It is important to see where these posts are so that you can build out your suite in an optimal way while, at the same time, incorporating them within the build-out so that they are completely hidden.

4. **Whether you have a ground floor or a second floor or higher** is an important factor to consider. All three of the offices that I have built have been on the second floor. First floor office suites are excellent locations as well, but I guess I just like the views from the top. You should consider the type of population you have coming into your office. For instance, if you have older patients that will be coming from the nearby retirement community, you may want to

be situated on the ground floor. In one of my offices, I had a choice between an adjacent suite next to the large anchor restaurant or the second floor; I chose the second floor. It worked out quite well since the adjacent suite always complains of smells coming from the restaurant, but I don't have any issues with it since I am on top. As far as exposure, a good number of people may walk in and out of the restaurant, but being on the second floor still gets you great visibility, so I wouldn't worry about it too much.

5. **Proximity to the elevator** is important because it's more convenient for patients to go to an office close to the elevator as opposed to walking long stretches of hallway.

6. **Your relation to other suites** in the building, especially if there are other dental offices, is critical. Be aware of the other business suites you are next to. In one of my locations, we are next to a physical therapy practice where there is a lot of foot traffic, which also helps raise awareness that there is a dentist nearby. Also realize that even if you are on the second floor and you are above a restaurant, you may have issues with different food-related aromas. I have a friend whose office is above a nice restaurant, but oftentimes he gets complaints about weird smells coming into his suite.

SIGNAGE

I love talking about signage! It is a hot topic in dentistry. Why? Because most dentists have the same signs up. Now, I am not referring to the doctor's name on the door of every medical and dental office. I'm talking about signage. C'mon, you know what I am talking about here. What you see at your dentist's office is the same exact sign as every other dentist's in the city. Want to know what the sign says? *"DENTIST"*! This is the most common signage for dentists. Signage, like this, that is not original puts your office in the negative before you even open for business. Oh wait, I forgot another sign that is really common: Dr. FirstName, LastName

D.D.S Dentistry. Why do dentists do this? I don't know what they are thinking, but I do know what they *should* be thinking!

One reason signage should not display your first and last name is that one day, hopefully not too long after you open, you'll have an associate dentist working with you. You want to market *the business* and not *you*; the best way to do this is to expose the business name. When you do it this way, patients will not just identify your name as the business, but they will see you inside that business entity. Plus, you'll have the option of hiring an associate who is *equally marketable as well*. If your sign says *"Dr. Jones, D.D.S.,"* then people will come in asking for Dr. Jones. When your sign is a *Doing Business As* (DBA) name, then you are marketing your brand *beyond just the scope of yourself*. Without swinging off on too much of a tangent here, a great book I would recommend for any business owner is *E-Myth Revisited* by Michael Gerber. Every dentist who runs (or plans to run) his or her own office should read this because it talks about building systems beyond the *scope* of your influence. This can only happen with the right identification: your signage.

HERE ARE THE THREE TYPES OF SIGNS YOU'LL WANT FOR YOUR PRACTICE:

1. **An external sign** should be placed outside the building above your suite location. Even though this is not always possible because of city restrictions and building requirements, I suggest you try to negotiate this into your lease.
2. **A monument sign** is an option if you can't place a sign on the actual building stucco wall. Monument signs are the ones you see perched on a grassy knoll or right in front of the parking lot of your building. My preference would always be to have an external sign on the building and a monument sign as well.
3. **A front office sign** is a great place to display your logo. An ideal location is the wall behind the reception area front desk. For

maximum effect, your office logo should be mounted on the wall behind your receptionist. A sign no larger than 4' x 6' should suffice.

If you are currently practicing in an office without a front office sign, spend some money and put one up. You'll see, it will make a presence, and it will give your front office a professional and striking appearance.

Your signage is the face of your brand; it's what your patients will become familiar with before they even walk into your office.

KEEP THESE POINTS IN MIND AS YOU DESIGN YOUR SIGNAGE:

Choose a DBA and incorporate this into your signage. Do not make it your first name and last name. A logo and image gives people a feeling about your practice well before they arrive. Do you want it to be fun and energetic, modern and chic, or cheerful with bold colors? Think of the type of practice you envision for yourself. Remember what we talked about in Chapter 1? None of these mental images resemble the all-encompassing *DENTIST* sign, right? At least, I hope not! Make all of those feelings of grandeur along with your personality come out in your signage. I live in southern California, and so I wanted my brand to have a happy, modern, and cheerful feel to it. That's why we called it *SoCal Smiles Dentistry*. Southern California is also known as *SoCal*, and it had a ring to it, so that's all it needed for it to work. You should think of a brand that expresses your vision for your practice. Make it simple, but make sure it captures your vision.

Also, make sure you file for use of that DBA. If you file for use of a specific DBA with the city, you have rights to use that business name without it infringing on anyone else's name. This is simple to do and can be done inexpensively online via LegalZoom.com.

Make a logo with your business name. If you are looking for an inexpensive way to get logo ideas and other input from hundreds of people, go to Crowdspring.com. Give the world your idea about what you want your logo to look like, and then sit back while a bunch of different logos come in for you to choose from.

Know the guidelines. External building signage often has some very rigid guidelines. Look at the signage program by your builder and the city. Hire a sign architect to design a sign using your logo, and make sure you put it on paper and over the floor so you can get a better idea of its size and the way it will look on the building.

Colors and lighting on your sign go well if done correctly. The key here is to make sure they don't look tacky and overdone.

Try the city. Even if, at first, the landlord tells you that you can't have a sign up on the building, ask why. If he or she says that the city will not allow it, then go to the city and fill out a building signage request. I once was told that I could not put a sign up on the building, but then the dentist below me had one up before he even moved in! It is worth the money to place a sign on a building that identifies your practice.

What now? You need to claim your territory, and it's more than just signing on the dotted line. You have to think about tomorrow—today. You are on your way to becoming a business tenant. Welcome to what could very well be your practice. It's just four walls right now, but it has the potential to be a lot more. But only if you promise to stay for ten years!

Chapter 3

LEASE NEGOTIATIONS

Give me a year of free rent, and I will give you ten years of occupancy.

Dentists are the best tenants! Once we are in, we never leave. We place so much money into improving the suite (and invest so much money in our education in order to practice dentistry, so the longer we remain tenants, the more our businesses grow). If I were a landlord, I would take that combo any day, so don't ever forget this when you negotiate your lease.

Negotiating a lease can be a very confusing and intense experience. Lease negotiations are one of the few times that you will be talking about something that may consistently impact you for seven or more years. As a dentist you've probably never negotiated a business lease. In fact, it is likely you may negotiate only one or two business leases your entire life.

CONSIDER THE FOLLOWING 3 POINTS AS YOU NEGOTIATE YOUR LEASE:

1. Monthly overhead costs and how your lease payment affects these costs each month.
2. How long you want to lease your suite with the possibility of renewing your lease.
3. Think of it as a long-term business plan. Will you sell your office within the next five years or keep it for over ten years?

Within these three points are a myriad of others you must also consider.

Below is a crash course in Real Estate 101 as it pertains to the build-out of your dental office. Most of this stuff is common sense but, if you don't know the terminology, it can be really confusing. I am going to outline some terminology that may be important to you when negotiating your lease. But I will outline it as it pertains to the build-out of your dental office because it will make you a much better negotiator who leverages these key points during your lease negotiations in order to get what you want.

In order to create your dream office and watch your business come to life, you must first familiarize yourself with some basic terminology. Within each definition are specific leverage points to help you negotiate your own lease, whether you are using an attorney or not. When you review and further negotiate your lease with the broker and landlord, you should discuss and negotiate all of these areas below. (Note: When looking over the following terms, *you or your corporation* will be identified as the *lessee* and the *landlord* as the *lessor*.)

21 POINTS OF NEGOTIATION FOR EVERY DENTAL OFFICE LEASE.

1. **Rentable square footage:** The total amount of square feet that you are renting for your dental office.

2. **Usable square footage:** The amount that you are allowed to build on. This number is almost always less than the rentable square footage. After the landlord determines the usable square footage, it is multiplied by the *load factor* of the building to determine the rentable area of the premises.

3. **Load factor:** The difference between the usable and the rentable square footage is exemplified by this term, and it is usually expressed as a percentage. For example, if the load factor is about 15 percent, then out of every hundred square feet, you will be able to build on only eight-five of those one hundred square feet. Even though you can only build on a lesser amount of the total square footage, you are still responsible for the rent on the total amount or total rentable square footage.

4. **TI allowance:** Depending on your location and building management, you may get money from the landlord to build out your office. Sounds great, right? Well, not all landlords and building locations handle build-outs this way. I suggest you highly favor the ones that do and avoid the ones that don't, unless it's a unique situation that you cannot pass up. Essentially, TI stands for *tenant improvement,* and the funds are allocated for this only. In other words, TI is how much money the landlord is willing to give you to build your office. This number can vary tremendously anywhere from no money to the cost of the entire build-out. This is usually given per square foot of the usable space.

5. **TI disbursement schedule:** The money that the landlord gives you in the form of TI allowance must be paid to you in a structured fashion. Generally, you won't get all of the funding up front, although you should request that you do. In the likely event that they don't, here is what a fair TI disbursement sequence might look like: one-third of the TI allowance could be paid when you get a *rough inspection* sign-off from the city. The second one-third of the TI allowance could be paid when you receive electrical services for the building or get the Temporary Certificate of Occupancy from the city. The last one-third of the TI allowance is usually paid when you receive the Final Certificate of Occupancy. You can always negotiate these terms

with the landlord, but this is usually beneficial for both sides. If your landlord agrees to pay you half or all of the TI allowance at the start of construction, this is even better since you have more money at the outset and greater control of fund disbursement.

6. **CAM charges or triple net (NNN) charges or operating expenses:** Overhead for the expenses incurred by the landlord to keep the building and surrounding areas in orderly and operable condition. The landlord will usually allocate an additional portion to your rent to be able to pay these expenses. Traditionally, they can be anywhere from ten cents to fifty-five cents and upward. The landlord is required to give you a thorough breakdown at the end of the year to show you how the CAM charges for your year were allocated. If they came up short on their estimate and the actual expenses were more than what they predicted, then you will have to pay them at the beginning of the following year along with your rent. If they overestimated the CAM charges for the year, you will be credited. Don't expect this one to happen too often.

   Also be aware of exclusions to common area operating expenses. The landlord should also lay out what is not considered a CAM expense. (You don't want to be in the position of finding out that the management is using your monthly CAM allocations to host parties that promote their building.) These exclusions should be presented to you in the lease or addendum so you know what is not covered in the expense allowance as well.

7. **Lease commencement date:** The date you will begin paying your rent and the date your lease will start from, which is negotiable depending on your build-out time, when you signed the lease, and the terms established during negotiations. Don't hesitate to ask to move this date back or even negotiate a lack of lower rent payments to an *extended lease commencement date* instead. A number of options and variations are available in all lease negotiations.

8. **Substantial completion:** An arbitrary term estimating the date most of your build-out will be complete or substantially completed. Please remember that this term is something that is negotiated and set by *you*. Substantial completion can mean when you get your

Final Certificate of Occupancy or even when all the furniture is in to start business, but it can also mean when the electricity gets turned on. *Substantial completion must be agreed upon and **defined** on your terms. Thus, it can be either a landmark time to start rent payments or to move forward with some other agreement you've arranged with the landlord. It is important that you define what "substantial completion" means prior to signing the lease.*

9. **Addendum:** Any written declaration in addition to the standard lease agreement as drafted by your landlord. Almost always you will find an addendum attached to the lease that is specific for your negotiations and your suite location. If you have verbally negotiated with the landlord, make sure it is reflected in the addendum. Remember that if it is not documented in the lease then, legally, no one is held accountable for it.

10. **Agreed use:** Signifies multispecialty dentistry. *Important:* Under this definition you can always add specialties later and, hence, avoid the landlord telling you that you cannot add a specialty because other specialties are already in the building.

11. **Base rent:** The rent that you pay, not including the CAM or operating expenses. *Important:* This rate will be the basis on which your annual rent increases.

12. **Annual base rent increase:** Usually, most leases have a pre-negotiated base rent increase annually after the first year. Note: In real estate, almost anything can be negotiated, this being one of them.

13. **Assignment/subletting:** It is important to have a vision for your office. Do you plan to sell it and, if so, when? What is the final destination for your business? You've got to be able to answer these questions with certainty because what is written here will influence the answers to the above questions. Keep these fine points in mind when coordinating your negotiations with the landlord:

   • The landlord will usually want a written notice if you plan to assign or sublease any part of your suite.
   • You may be held responsible for your entire lease term *even if you have assigned* the lease to a new buyer.

- If the new buyer of your practice (the one to whom you assigned the lease) defaults, the landlord will come after you and hold you primarily responsible. I wasn't aware of this until recently when, under the terms of one of my leases, I am liable for the business success of another tenant/dentist to whom I sold my office, even though the landlord approved that tenant prior to signing the lease. This is important since, ideally, you don't want to be liable after you sell your place.

- You should be able to sublet a portion of space in your office. Let's say, for example, that you have an oral surgeon who wants to pay you rent for a couple of rooms twice a month and work in your office. This rent payment for the use of your office should go directly to you, the owner. However, many lease terms stipulate that if you get paid more than the rent amount, the landlord gets 50 percent of that excess portion. Most of the time, this not an issue since you are not going to collect more than the amount of your rent. If you anticipate collecting more than the amount of your rent, you should negotiate this clause down to less than 50 percent. In a nutshell, you should clarify that you can sublet your suite to other specialties at will.

14. **Temporary Certificate of Occupancy (TCO):** A certificate that you must receive for construction to commence in your suite. Usually, this will occur after you've already had a rough inspection of the suite and the contractor has completed some framing. Every city will have different provisions, and some cities will be more lenient than others. This can also indicate that you are approved for further, more involved construction of your suite.

15. **Final Certificate of Occupancy:** The *final* is given when your electrical services have begun and you are almost ready to go. A city representative will do a walk-through of your suite and check for any electrical hazards, door frame concerns, handicap regulations, HVAC improvements, properly illuminated exit signs, and any other regulatory improvements that may not be up to city code. You can open up for business after this has been granted.

16. **Space planning:** The phase in which you design and plan the layout of your office prior to construction and submission of plans to the city for approval.

17. **Construction management fee:** This fee is created by the lessor so that he or she can pay for a construction manager on the job site. Most lessors will have a superintendent or construction manager overseeing the project. Two of my leases read the following: *"Lessee shall pay the fee of Lessor's Construction Manager in an amount equal to three (3%) of the total cost of the Tenant Improvements, including all soft costs such as architect's, engineer's and permit fees (the "Construction Manager Fee") which payment shall be made by way of Lessor's deduction of said fee from the Tenant Improvement Allowance to be paid by Lessor to Lessee."* Phew! Now, that's a mouthful! In layman's terms, this means that you must pay the construction manager 3 percent of your total cost to build the place; that 3 percent will be deducted from the TI allowance that the landlord is supposed to pay you. This is definitely not a good position to be in since, if it costs you $200,000 in tenant improvements, then you must pay the construction manager (the landlord, as far as you're concerned) $6,000. Since you are building out, you will probably visit it quite often and notice anything that you want changed or is not going as planned. The construction manager is not worth a ton of money, especially if you will be overseeing the whole project. The better way to do this is to first try and eliminate any fee to the construction manager since you will be the one on the job site frequently overseeing the project. If this attempt fails with your landlord, place a cap on the fee. You can propose 2 percent or 3 percent, or whatever percentage, with a total cap not to exceed a certain amount such as $2,000–$3,000. This way, your fee doesn't depend on tenant improvement costs; it has a ceiling.

18. **Demising wall:** This is the wall that separates your suite from the neighboring suite. Since walls always have two sides, you must inquire and negotiate who will drywall your side of that wall—you or the landlord? Sometimes the demising wall is not even put up within the suite, so this may be a point of negotiation between you and your landlord. Negotiate the landlord constructing this wall according to

his or her provisions. You can then split the cost of putting drywall on *your side* or, if you are really convincing, have the landlord pay for the construction of the wall *and* the drywall that goes on your side. This is a fairly straightforward issue and can save you a few thousand dollars in construction, so I highly recommend that you carefully negotiate the demising wall.

19. **Sheer wall:** A wall that can't be moved, relocated, or cut down but can be located within your suite anywhere designated by the building construction laws. This is an important consideration because it may create a design challenge as you cannot terminate or modify the dimensions of that wall.

20. **Mechanics lien:** Also known as a construction lien. This helps the contractor enforce payment of the amount owed. Essentially this is a security interest or title to your build-out. For instance, if the contractor put all of his time and expense into building your office and then you don't pay him his last portion at the end of the build-out, they could hold the assets of your business or building liable for the unpaid portions. Every time you make a payment to your contractor you should have them sign a "lien release form" that indicates you paid them and you are free of any liabilities. This applies for subcontractors(usually working below the general contractor) as well. For instance, if the general contractor doesn't pay the subcontractors you should not be held liable for this non-payment. The way to protect yourself is to have all contractors sign lien releases.

21. **Personal guarantee:** This basically states that you are personally responsible for the success of your practice and anything related to it for the entire term of your lease. Some basic provisions for your lease will require you to identify who the lease is between. Is it you or your corporation? Is there is personal guarantee? I recommend that you place your lease between the landlord and your corporation, without a personal guarantee backed by you as an individual. Put another way, you are not your business. You must always think of your business as another entity, an item in and of itself.

These are all of the terms you really need to know in order to negotiate your lease effectively. Yes, you can take this task through grand proportions of meticulous detail, but these items will still remain the anchor points for securing your lease. After reading the twenty-one points, you may still think of them as separate, unrelated items. Let's take a few minutes to tie it all together so that you can appreciate its value and really understand where we are going.

Let's summarize the above points in a sequence that is likely to unfold as you negotiate your lease. First, you will search for your location either with the help of a local commercial real estate agent or by driving around town in the most ideal areas you'd like to practice. I found two of my three office locations by simply driving around to areas that I knew I would like to be in, and many of my colleagues have done the same. After you find your locations, contact the listing agent and begin negotiating your lease. Ask the agent a few of the following questions:

- What is the base rent and CAM charge?
- What is the total square footage of the space? The load factor?
- What is the lease term? Is there an option to re-lease and at what value?
- What is the TI allowance for the suite?
- What is the lease commencement date?

Also, ask the age of the building and when the building will be ready to occupy and be built out for your practice. After your questions have been answered satisfactorily, you must then coordinate a meeting with the landlord, yourself, and your agent. The goal of this meeting should be a productive discussion that addresses the other pertinent topic areas we highlighted in the twenty-one points. This is a good time to review estimated build-out time, aiming for around four to six months after signing the lease. Now is the appropriate time to discuss commencing the lease and paying rent.

Another important issue to resolve at this meeting is the amount of the TI allowance: the more the better! Always aim to get the most possible and as much of it upfront as you can. As I mentioned above, you can also divide it into *thirds* with certain building landmarks as reference points to distribute the funds. It is not uncommon to get $50–$70 per square foot to build out your place. Just recently a landlord offered me a "turn key" TI. This is when the landlord builds out your entire suite at no cost to you, and you simply just have to install the equipment. Imagine how this would decrease your build-out costs. *I wouldn't even step into a build-out that doesn't offer a significant TI allowance.* The reason I am emphasizing this point is that I want you to know that it's okay to push for more money from the landlord to build your suite. By developing the inside of his or her building, you are assuring your landlord that you will likely be there for a long time. In consideration of this, ask for as much TI allowance as you can!

Lastly, talk about construction and designate responsibility for structures such as the demising wall. Suggest that the landlord pay to construct and drywall both sides of the wall. Remember, this is the wall that separates your suite from the neighboring one. If it is not up yet, have them build it and drywall it; if it is already up, have them drywall your side. In addition, identify all structural posts and sheer walls within the suite so you know which walls inside the suite need to stay and which ones you can remove, if any.

In closing, make sure you also minimize any other extraneous fees, such as the construction management fee, the way we detailed above. Reassure the landlord that you are committed to your project's success as it will be your main source of income and livelihood. Reconfirm your commitment, and emphasize that you will not give a personal guarantee for more than one year. Remind them that the lease will be signed by your business entity and not by you personally.

After you've agreed to the terms of the lease and have signed on the dotted line for years to decades, you're ready to build your home. Remember that it's not just a place to go to work; rather, it's an immaculate practice unlike anything your patients have ever seen.

Now let's begin to understand the...

Chapter 4

PSYCHOLOGY OF A WORLD-CLASS OFFICE DESIGN

Whenever you design something, don't settle for anything less then a masterpiece.

Now that you have successfully negotiated your lease, what's next? You need to have a vision of what your office will look like when it is all completed. How is it going to feel to your patients when they walk in? What is it going to convey to your patients before anyone even says a word to them. Your office needs to have a presence and one that says your brand and team are a magnificent combination of dentistry and dental health. You want your patients to feel as if they just stepped into the best office in the world *ever! Your office is a work of art; never design anything less than an art piece.* Don't make your office just average; make it world-class, and make it say something about who you are and the standards you keep in our field as a professional and as a person. Be immaculate.

Dentistry is the artful designing of your patients' smiles, and your office is the place of work for this art. I love it when so many of our patients comment on how gorgeous the office looks and how they have never been to a dental office that looks like ours. One of the practices is located on the second floor on a busy section of a major street in the city of Tustin. We have towering windows and keep the shades open all the time. One of our patients came into the office because he was driving down the street in his Lamborghini and noticed our ceiling effects and unique office colors and said he just had to come in and check us out to see what services we offered. He said that he was intrigued by the cool-looking colors and office design. I thought, *All this from just driving by?* He and his entire family became regular patients of ours and, when I got to know him better, he revealed that he designed custom homes for celebrity clients such as Arnold Schwarzenegger and Jackie Chan. Obviously, he had an eye for design, and this is what brought him in. Who would have thought that a patient would be driving by in his Lamborghini and stop to see the dentist *because* he noticed it *while driving?* This is all about the design.

I share this story to express how important the design elements are in constructing your office. Your vision for your practice breeds its design, so let's tap into the psychology of a world-class practice design. When your patients walk through the door of your office, what is it that they notice first? Is it a wall, the front desk, or the waiting room chairs?

It's none of these things *alone; rather,* it's all of these things together that paint a picture, framing your office and brand.

The first thing you will notice about most dental offices is that they are built in a very claustrophobic manner, to the point that you may even say they are small clutters with chairs and sterilization areas that are just carelessly grouped together! Not only are they very close together as if someone tried to cram a bunch of dental chairs in a small area but they have cords, trays, and suction tips coming at the patient from a front-delivery system.

The points below have an enormous impact on a winning psychological layout in the office. *The most important aspect of a winning design psychology is to make your office non-intimidating.* Everything I do in my office caters to this idea. Making your office comfortable is different from making it non-intimidating. Comfort, seeks to please with amenities whereas a non-intimidating environment reassures patients, provides them with a sense of safety, and instills in them confidence. In a dental office, reassuring your patients is much more effective than throwing costly little amenities at them. When you are at home, you are confident and reassured that you are safe, so make sure your patients feel the same way about your office. The methods and techniques in this chapter are psychological cues you can use to help your patients feel safe and confident as they enter your office.

One of the reasons why impressive-looking offices have an immaculate *presence* is that the layout incorporates a winning psychology. Before you sit down with your architect or space planner to draft up preliminary designs, you need to have clear vision in your mind's eye of what you want your office to look like when it's all completed—from the front door to each dental chair.

After building three world-class offices and having thousands of patients comment and provide feedback on our office design, I have learned quite a lot about what works and what doesn't. *So, whether you are building out or modifying your existing office, keep these eight keys in mind.*

8 KEYS TO A WORLD-CLASS DENTAL OFFICE DESIGN

1. **Always go with a rear-delivery system.** This is a system that extends from the rear of the dental chair. It doesn't scare the patient by coming right at them, so it is much less intimidating. The only exception to this rule is your hygiene chairs which, if you really want, can be a front-delivery system. The reason I say this is that most people are not afraid of going to get their teeth cleaned but are more than a little nervous about other treatments.

2. **Always place a computer screen in front of the patient.** I prefer to mount them on the wall because the type that comes off the chair is nice, but a wall-mounted screen is more aesthetic and leaves

plenty of foot space for patients of all heights. Remember, a spacious, yet vibrant operatory is a good thing.

3. **Always place a window in front of your dental chair.** The dental chair is where you make your money, so wouldn't it make sense to place it in front of another non-intimidating feature such as a big window? Some dentists like to reserve their windows for their offices, or for overlooking the sterilization areas or even the front office. But windows are best used in front of or within the dental operatory.

4. **Try to place windows in your reception area.** Remember, windows in the dental treatment rooms take priority over windows in the reception area. The second priority for window placement is, of course, the reception area.

5. **Create interesting ceiling effects throughout the office.** Don't think of your ceiling as the top part of your suite. Ceiling effects can add a unique look and presence to your practice, and ceilings are perfect for displaying something creative, such as indirect lighting and drop down drywall ceiling effects. People prefer to be in places that elicit happiness and optimism. In this case, we are talking about patients' health as well as their smile. *If you are going to enhance someone's smile, shouldn't you also inspire them TO smile?* Think of that for a minute. Also, think about the other design elements patients will see when they first walk in, such as the contours of the office and indirect lighting. We will dive more into this later on.

6. **Use color to influence your patients.** Aren't people more likely to buy from you if they are in a confident and happy state of mind? Paint color is one of the most powerful and cost-effective ways to set the tone of the office.

7. **Design the reception area with style.** Think of the reception area as if it were the entry to a luxury hotel. It is not just a waiting room; it is the first point of influence, and it will set the mood of your patients before they ever see you. It's important that the reception area must be clean, but most dentists forget those small details that can really make a difference. Below is a checklist of tips for reception area design.

RECEPTION AREA DESIGN

✓ **Make your reception area front desk the focal point of service:** In other words, the origination and final destination of all patient traffic should be your reception area front desk. Make it easy for patients to hang out there because the front desk is where your staff is going to communicate and connect with them. When new patients walk in and observe your team interacting with your patients, what they see should breed a sense of comfort. An effective office layout with a well-designed reception area will communicate just that.

✓ **Always place at least one couch** in the front office. A comfortable couch conveys a welcoming, your-home-is-my-home feeling.

✓ **The front desk should have an open view** so that your reception area team can make eye contact with patients coming in and patients sitting down.

✓ **Place non-dental artwork in the reception area** that has nothing to do with dentistry or dental health. This is important since dental art is not what patients really want to see; instead, they want to look at creative decor. It is well worth spending a little money on creative artwork displays for the reception area.

✓ **Have a coffee table.** This gives it a homey feel, and patients will subconsciously feel more comfortable when they step into your office.

✓ **Have books and other educational material** on the coffee table about your industry and cool, important facts.

✓ **Have a "testimonials" book in the reception area.** Provide solid, encouraging testimonials about your team, procedures, and your ability and expertise as a dentist. If you have one, use the TV in your reception area for video testimonials and before and after pictures.

✓ **Use an iPad or a media tablet** in your reception area to play video testimonials and display other important office information. The advent of the iPad has been so influential in communicating messages through videos and graphics. You can have your iPad set to your office's YouTube channel that plays videos on commonly ask dental questions and concerns. Your video can also inform patients through valuable information on the variety of products and services you offer.

✓ **Have a surround sound ceiling audio system with upbeat music.** Your music should brand your thinking about dentistry, life, and people in general. I would avoid any extremes in musical art. Be people- and family-friendly, yet keep it real with some contemporary music.

✓ **Use a healthy and vibrant mix of colors in your office.** Below, we will discuss colors in detail since they can leave an imprint of vibrancy and success on your patients.

✓ **DO NOT use outdated, office-like chairs** in the reception area like those used in the older medical establishments. Also, don't arrange your chairs into something that resembles an assembly line row; this is the most disgusting and outdated elements of design to have in your front office. Change things up, and keep a comfortable amount of space between chairs, couches, or sectionals in your reception area.

✓ **No food in the reception area.** Have a staff lounge and make it office policy to use it daily. The front desk is not a kitchen table, nor is it a beverage bar.

8. **Think of your office restroom as you would your luxury home bathroom.** It may sound crazy, but how you design and maintain your office restroom says a lot about how you run your entire business. If your restroom is cold, damp, and dingy, then patients will expect similarly of your office. A restroom also conveys pride in ownership. Give your patients some credit; they know that if owners care about the state of the restroom, they must also care about the overall cleanliness of the entire office. A clean, comfortable restroom gives patients confidence in the overall environment, including the quality of the services you offer.

RESTROOM DESIGN

✓ **Place the paper towels** in a tray or basket.

✓ **Ensure the bathroom door opens to the sink, not to the toilet.** When patients open the door, the first thing in their line of sight should be the sink and not the toilet. I made this mistake in one of my offices.

✓ **Always have plenty of soap** in the bathroom.

✓ **Keep hand lotion** in your bathroom—maybe even some mints.

✓ **Have some toothbrushes** and sample-size toothpaste tubes.

✓ **Display artwork** in your bathroom. That's right. Just do it and you'll thank me later!

In the three offices that I have built, I have used all eight of these world-class keys, which has helped me to achieve the immaculate presence that I've been talking about. I am now going to focus on two of those keys—color and ceiling effects—in more detail because they are absolutely necessary to create an extraordinary ambience in your office. Color and ceiling effects influence how people visually evaluate your office. *As you will soon learn, color creates a powerful energy within your office, and ceiling effects complement your office design, giving it an artful distinction.*

COLOR

Color is a topic that I am definitely passionate about. The most effective way to enhance your office's appearance is through the use of color; it's not through installing granite countertops in the reception area or even flat-screen TVs everywhere, but instead through the use of color on *specific* walls for various wall effects. By choosing the right colors, you can change someone's mood in an instant. If you don't believe me, think of a time you went into your closet and picked out an outfit or shirt based on how you were feeling. I do it all the time, and the colors we choose and see make us *feel* different, affect our moods and, at times, ignite some very specific emotions as well.

Dentists still don't get this! Take a look, for example, at the walls of most medical and dental offices; I think you'd find on them every possible shade of white. After all, who made the rule that health care offices had to don sterile, washed out white walls? We live and breathe in color. So, why wouldn't you use color on your walls?

Each color has emotion and thought patterns attached to it. Think of a red dollar bill. Sounds a bit outrageous, right? How about a green one-hundred dollar bill? Now this sounds like something you'd want. If green means go, then red means what? It means *stop*. Someone may look at purple and gold and think of the Los Angeles Lakers, whereas another may see blue and think of the endless sky. Various studies have been done on how certain colors initiate buying actions. You should be using colors to express the essence of your practice's vision and goals. I wanted my own offices to express a cutting edge, clean, vibrant, happy, and cheerful energy, which is why I chose the colors I did. I created an environment that supports my patients and puts them in a positive state of mind when we are planning their treatment, discussing finances, and scheduling future appointments. Their mood affects these important decisions, so why not put them in the best place or the *best state possible?* Before they've experienced you and your office, the colors you choose will influence their mood while they wait in the reception area. Color makes it possible for them to *feel* your office immediately as they walk through your doors. Look at all the ways color has impacted *you* and *your* decisions.

Now, here is the exciting part. Think of your office as if it were a blank canvas with infinite possibilities for creating any emotions and thought patterns you want! Knowing what you now know about color, why not use colors that support your business environment and are conducive for motivating your patients and influencing their decisions about their treatment plans?

From the colors I've listed below, create variations and color schemes based on your preference. Each color conveys a different emotion, so it is important that you consider the feeling your practice gives your patients the instant they walk in.

Yellow = knowledge, energy, joy, intellect, and youth. This is a great color to place in your back office as you want to give patients vibrancy and a feeling of knowledge as you are interacting with them clinically.

Blue=knowledge, trust, tranquility, calmness, peacefulness, and coolness. Blue is my favorite color! This is a great color to use in the reception area, especially in the transitional area that leads your patients to the back office and treatment rooms. Don't overuse blue since it may take away from the vibrancy of your office.

Green=fertility, wealth, healing, success, and growth. Green is a great color to use in select areas of your office. I suggest lighter shades of green, almost like a sea green or light mint green. This will give that healing, wealthy, and rich appearance you want your winning design to convey.

Orange=creativity, invigoration, uniqueness, and stimulation. Shades of orange are extremely effective. I have used shades of orange in all of my offices because it endorses creativity and invigorates the imagination. You want your patients to feel that they are in a creative place for their smile design. You will be designing smiles, and your office design must convey that. I prefer placing shades of orange on higher wall areas such as soffits and ceilings.

Red=passion, anger, vigor, love, and danger. Red is a powerful color, so you should use all shades of it in limited quantities. In one of our offices, I have one curved wall that is a lighter shade of red and a few small accent walls with that color. It will give your practice a sense of flare and attitude with an edge.

Light brown=peace, earthliness, warmth, and sincerity. This is a great color to have in multiple areas of your office. You can't lose with shades of light brown, such as taupe, light coffee, and caramel. Use this color generously on multiple walls.

White=purity, healing, perfection, cleanliness, and virtue. I would keep the majority of your ceiling white or ultra-pure white. It will give your practice a feeling of higher ceilings and less noticeable ceilings. White also goes well with any other color, such as orange, that you may have on other parts of the ceiling.

Vanilla is also a good color choice because it can be mixed with bolder colors, such as orange and blue, which will give your office a more contemporary look. A good substitute for white, vanilla is my color of choice when it comes to neutral walls with no color.

The most *influential* area in your office to use the right colors is your reception area. Devote some time to choosing color combinations that your patients will *feel* and appreciate when they first walk in. What color are the soffit, the back wall, and the other walls in the rest of your office? In our office, the ceiling is ultra-pure white and the non-colored walls are painted a shade called vanilla custard. As a patient, you would assume that this is a nice office by the appearance of the reception area alone. Patients don't care whether your office has A-dec chairs; they do, however, care about the way your office looks.

Let's look at a few office designs and evaluate them based on what we've already talked about.

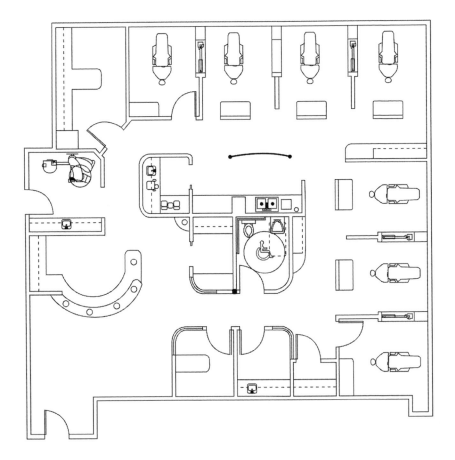

Diagram 1

This is a beautiful multi-specialty, seven-chair office. The following points make this design a total winner:

- Here we have an open, non-intimidating design and layout. Take a look at the front and back offices. No doors separate the front office and back office, yet privacy is maintained through effective line of sight and detailed architecture. When patients walk into this office, they feel as if there is nothing to hide. This layout also provides some intrigue because, as you walk through the open entrance, more of the office is revealed as the walkway curves.
- The treatment rooms are not cluttered with cabinetry and dental equipment. All the equipment is nestled away in a twelve o'clock position.
- Two-way x-ray units housed in bifold cabinets partition each room.
- Two entrances and two exits from the front and back offices due to the loop-around design make this layout ideal. It's important to note that not every office will have this type of design, but the ones that do give way for amazing setups and a comfortable ambience.
- Two closed rooms could be used for patients who require more privacy or need procedures such as pedodontics and oral surgery. These rooms could also be reserved for those challenging patients that you don't want scaring away other patients.
- The back door entrance used by staff members and doctors.
- For patients with quick appointments, the panorex is located in the front of the office.
- The focal point is the reception area as there are no doors that separate the front and back offices, and the two entrances and exits originate and terminate there, respectively.

Now, let's evaluate another layout.

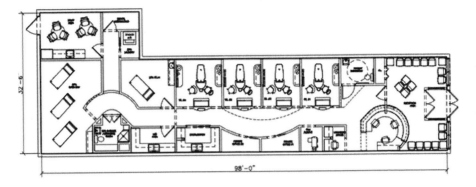

Diagram 2

THE POSITIVES:

- A second entry door is available for staff members and doctors.
- The bathroom is located toward the front of the office, which means easy access for patients waiting in the reception area.

THE NEGATIVES:

- When you walk into this office, it's as if you are stepping into a box. The front doors open and you are immediately closed off from the back office. I am not a big fan of this setup because it doesn't conform to the open, non-intimidating design we discussed above.
- There are no windows in this suite!
- Notice how all the chairs are lined up against the wall. Whatever you do, don't keep these types of chairs in your reception area! Almost everyone uses them, and they are so impersonal. Place a couch in there, as well as some nice plush chairs that you would use in your own house. Remember, the couch gives it a warm and welcoming feel. I also hate the fact that patients have to walk down a straight aisle to access the entire office.
- The front door is the only entrance and exit. Your office should have a nice open flow to it. It is hard for this space to be designed that

way because it's more of a rectangle; it's wide from right to left and short from top to bottom.

- You don't need a sink in every room. This particular office has one, but it doesn't mean you must design your office the same way.
- X-ray units are in all four general operatories. You can cut your cost by half by having x-rays that swing to the right and left allowing them to go between both operatories. This is something to consider when building your office since it can save you money and also space.

CEILING EFFECTS

Let's talk about ceilings. The ceiling space of your suite is important because it provides visual cues and adds to the overall appearance and presence of your office. Ever been to a cathedral where the ceilings were all grand and colorful? Didn't it give you a different feel altogether? You want your ceilings to do the same, but you also want to convey a warmth and welcomeness with a dash of confidence.

Your ceiling will likely consist of one of two basic ceiling design options. The first is called T-Bar, and it is the most common type of ceiling. You've seen them before; they are the white twenty-four square-inch tiles found in most offices. Your ceiling will have a basic look, but the tiles are inexpensive and provide easy access to the components and wiring above.

The second ceiling design option is drywall. It looks much nicer and can be painted any color since it's basically what a regular room wall is made of. Drywall ceilings are more expensive, but not by much. Drywall ceilings have canned lighting or even an indirect light source, and they can add to your ceiling the illusion of height or step elements. Making use of your ceiling will give your office a brand new personality. How many times have we been to an office location or even a home and noticed that the ceiling is just a plain popcorn ceiling or a stained up T-bar? So, choose variations in ceiling modality and color that offset the rest of your office decor; such changes will give your office distinction.

Here is a ceiling plan of that same office space from Diagram 1:

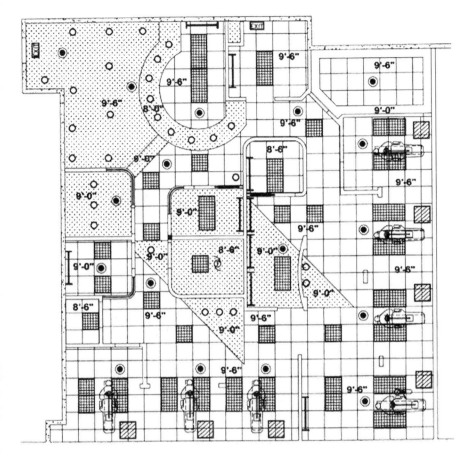

Diagram 1- Ceiling Plan

Although the ceiling plan is basic, it looked great when the office was all built out. Notice that the ceilings for the drywall are a different height than the T-bar. This height effect made for an interesting three-dimensional appearance throughout the suite. Look at how the three triangles protrude at the T-bar throughout the back office. Put some thought into your ceiling effects because they will really give your suite that touch of elegance. You want people to come into your office and comment on the details; in fact, it's all about those details, and there is no better way than to impress them with the subtle uniqueness of your ceiling plan.

Let's look at another plan and review some of its important build-out elements.

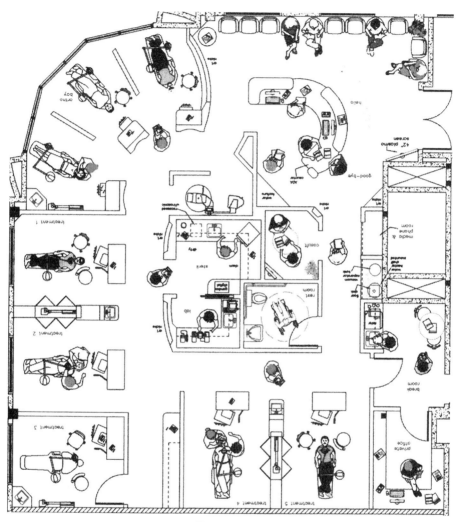

Diagram 3

Here are 15 key points to take away from this build out design.

- When you walk in, you are standing seven to ten feet away from the reception area front desk.

- You didn't walk into a waiting room that looks like a box. Accentuating curves and semi-circular structural elements give it dimension. The design is far from a typical dental office. Place a nice couch against the wall on the left and some chairs around the circular areas. There is a lot of potential with this layout.

- Do you see the wall behind the front desk? It gives the front desk some presence and a subtle authority. These qualities are great when scheduling patients and talking about treatment.

- The two entrances and exits provide a loop design, which is great since it gives you more than one way to come and go in your office.

- Back door access for staff and doctors gives you and your staff some privacy.

- A twelve o'clock setup for all dental chairs eliminates an intimidating front-delivery system. Patients love this since instruments and tray setups are out of sight.

- The private room could be reserved for pedo and surgical cases.

- The floor-to-ceiling windows in every room offer a pleasant view and give an open and relaxing effect to patients when seated in the room. Windows also eliminate any sense of claustrophobia that can occur by just being in a dental office.

- The doctor's office and staff lounge are in one area, promoting team cohesion. This also ensures that your staff stays productive as you can monitor what they are doing with your time. Yes, it's *your* time since you are paying them. Office design can also promote productivity!

- The restroom is situated toward the front of the office suite and away from the treatment areas.

- The sterilization and lab area is centrally located. Notice that the lab also has a sliding door that you can close to eliminate noise from model trimmers, vacuum machines, and other equipment pieces that may cause a lot of noise.

- No doors separate the front office from the back office. Yet, there is full privacy between the two by the angulated design that plays on the line-of-sight elements we've incorporated. In other words, the contours and height of the walls block views to the back office.

- No excess cabinetry clutters your operatories.
- Private consultation room for staff and patients to discuss treatment options.
- The x-ray units that swing between two rooms eliminate the need to buy x-ray units for every room.

You must be clear on how you want your office to look in order to have a successful build-out. Utilize the eight keys to office design, and your office will come together like a beautiful, well-planned masterpiece. Now that you have a grand vision for your office design, all we have to do is hire some help to make it all come together. You must form the best team to help you build your practice. Let's hire some contractors!

Chapter 5

HAMMER TO NAIL

*It's time to use the tools you've got to build your office,
but who are you gonna get to hold the hammer?*

Y ou are now ready to learn how to build a dental office that you've always envisioned. First, let's walk through an outline of what you can expect as the designing, planning, and the construction begin. I am going to make this really simple for you. The biggest organizational challenge that I had was that I didn't know where to start. In this section, I will show you exactly where you should start to get things moving forward. Once you gain some momentum, you'll also gain the confidence you need to move forward with construction.

In this chapter we will learn the following:

- The best way to get your office designed and how to choose the person who will draft up and coordinate the design process
- How to choose the right contractor to build your practice and factors to consider when choosing a contractor

- How to pay your contractor through the course of the construction process
- The overall construction sequence and timeline

The *number one rule* you should keep in mind is to hire someone who has designed dental office suites before. Don't be tempted to hire the stellar architect who has designed impressive buildings and homes but has not yet designed a dental office. Using experienced contractors will ensure your project runs more efficiently. Moreover, you'll be confident that they can give you some sound advice when you need it most.

3 WAYS TO GET YOUR SUITE DESIGNED

1. **Call your local dental supply companies** such as Patterson Dental, Pearson Dental, or Henry Shein. These are the three big ones. They all have dental office design specialists on board who can design your suite from start to finish. They'll probably charge a nominal fee to design it as long as you purchase most of the equipment from them. The phrase *most of the equipment* could even have a dollar amount associated with it such as $50,000–$75,000 worth of equipment that must be purchased from them; your suite design will then be free. If you purchase equipment elsewhere, their design fee can range anywhere from $1.75 per square foot all the way up to $4 per square foot. If you are looking at a 2,500 square foot office, you're looking at $5,000 to $10,000 just for a design! This is a hefty price tag.

They might also charge you a flat fee up front with no contract for purchasing equipment. This fee can range anywhere from $2,000 to $3,000. Your freedom to decide which vendor to purchase equipment from makes this a great option. Anyone who purchases equipment from the big equipment companies holds tremendous negotiating power. They really want to work with you to make your office the office of your dreams and, as long as you're intelligent about leveraging this fact, it can prove to be a very effective business transaction.

2. **Get an architect from your landlord** to help you design the suite. The landlord might suggest the building architect that designed the building itself. This is a great option as well; you may be able to negotiate a landlord-assisted design when you sign your lease. It is possible to include your design fee just by the fact that you are signing the lease. Remember that everything is negotiable. You will be the landlord's customer, client, tenant, or whatever you want to call it for the next seven to ten years just by signing a lease. Your landlord will want to help you build out a world-class office.

3. **Have your contractor design your suite.** So, here you are doing things a little backward, but it works just fine. You can grab a few contractors and have them come out to your suite and put together a preliminary design. If you like what you see, then go with it and have them bid on your project. If you don't like what the contractor put together, then present it to another contractor and have him or her develop different elements that will improve the office design.

Whether it's through your equipment provider, the landlord's architect, or a dental office contractor, the design must be completed before you can move on to the next step. After the design is completed, you are ready to select a contractor. Obviously, if your contractor is the one designing your suite, you have consolidated these two steps. But in order to choose a contractor, you must discuss cost with a few of them, get to know how they think, and figure in the various elements of the build-out. The office design that you have worked so hard on with your architect or design expert will now be used as an evaluation tool contractors will use to submit their bids. So, how do you go about choosing a winning contractor for your project?

CHOOSING THE RIGHT CONTRACTOR

The materials used to build your office are pretty much the same no matter what contractor you use. You'll need metal framework, drywall, plumbing pipes, air/vacuum piping, and electrical wiring. It's the same materials across the board, so why is there a $50,000–$100,000 difference in pricing among contractors? They want more money from you. It's that simple. Never go with the cheapest guy in town, nor should you hire the most expensive. My suggestion is to use someone who is very competitive in pricing and realistic in build-out goals. Haven't you heard the horror stories of contractors enthusiastically starting a job after winning the bidding war because they gave the best price, but actually underpriced the project and then couldn't afford to finish it? They jumped ship, leaving the dentist to go find another contractor to start where they left off. This is a nightmare, and it can be extremely expensive to fix.

Below I've listed ways to select a contractor who will give you a competitive price, build, and finish your office. The goal is to build your practice within two weeks of your projected build-out time.

THE 5 MOST IMPORTANT THINGS YOU MUST DO WHEN PICKING A DENTAL CONTRACTOR

1. **Interview five contractors but get to know three of them.** Make at least five copies of your design, and use them to do these things: interview at least five contractors and pick at least three to research. Got it? Don't go with the first guy you meet and think you've got a good price because a friend of yours built his office out around that price as well. Contractors will look over your design and usually take about one or two weeks to come up with a bid for your build-out. During this time, meet with and send it to other contractors as well. It is best to meet them at your job site and show them the building and suite; don't just give them office designs alone. Sometimes contractors will spot problem areas that may come up before they give you a bid. So, if you want a more accurate and realistic evaluation, always show them your suite before you give it to them to bid.

2. Evaluate bids side by side. As the bids start rolling in, you may notice one or two of them that are totally out of your price range, maybe even $100,000 higher than the next contractor. Get competitive! It's okay to negotiate how much you want to pay. Break down your price structure to cost per square foot. Competitive pricing can be anywhere from $55 to $85 per square foot. When evaluating pricing, use the following guidelines:

Framing: Consult your landlord for framing requirements before giving the contractor the go-ahead. Ask whether the metal studs are at twelve inches or sixteen inches, and discuss what type of insulation will be used within the wall cavity.

Ceiling: What type of ceiling was quoted in the price? Is it drywall or T-bar ceiling tile? How high is the ceiling from the ground floor? What does your building code require? A ten-foot-high ceiling is ideal. These are just a few of the questions you'll want to ask before deciding on a ceiling type.

Electrical: What type of lighting will your contractor provide? Light soffits and light effects should be included in your lighting plan. What are your power receptacles like? What color are they, and how many are there? You should be able to provide power drops wherever you need them. Remember that in your new dental office, modern, high-tech equipment requires power. Do you have an outlet under that sterilizer so no one sees wires everywhere?

Plumbing: Choose the sinks that you want in between treatment rooms. Are the standard sinks that are included with the contractor's bid attractive enough to place in your office? These plumbing fixtures should always add to the elegance of your office. Always inquire about these details since costs add up quickly as you choose looks or decor. Have you met all the requirements under the handicap code set by the city for dental offices? Will your contractor charge more if you decide to place and plumb your suite so that the housing for the compressor and vacuum system is located on the rooftop? This is an important feature that you have to negotiate with your landlord. To eliminate noise and free up space within your suite, ask your landlord to allow you to place the compressor and vacuum on the rooftop.

Mechanical: All air ducts, heating, air setup, and fans must be in the proper locations. Air flow and circulation in every room has to be balanced, so make sure your contractor includes an air-balance service and inspection for adequate ventilation in rooms with larger windows, which may require more air conditioning or heating due to the temperature range in those areas.

Fire: Know the fire sprinkler plan and where the fire extinguishers are located. Where are the ceiling fire sprinklers located? Are they concealed or jutting out of the ceiling? This plan will be largely dictated by the city and building code requirements, so check that your contractor is in compliance with these codes as well as the landlord's specifications. The last thing you want is to be deep in construction when your contractor tells you that it's a few thousand dollars extra for something your *landlord requires.* So, clarify your expectations from the beginning.

Cabinetry: This will be the most costly expense in all of your build-out. Most dentists overdo the cabinetry in their suites. What kind of cabinetry is the contractor providing? Is the bid for plastic laminate cabinetry? You should have the option of choosing color and making reasonable revisions. Will granite be included here? You should be very clear about your cabinetry plan for your entire office, and be certain how much space you need allocated for the different cabinet types. Remember to include cabinet space in your office for storing different products that may take more room, such as bottles of peridex or even large paper towels.

I recommend using a twelve o'clock setting for all of your operatories, so this would mean placing your cabinetry behind the patient's head if you imagine them reclining in the chair. Most offices have cabinets on both the left and right side of each treatment room, which is unnecessary; in fact, you end up having a room that looks too clinical. When it comes to cabinetry, remember to *keep it simple.* Sometimes your contractor will even suggest more cabinets, but you can explain why you don't need them. It's the exact opposite of what you want. Your treatment room should look clean, modern, and inviting.

Door: What types of doors would best suit your office? Solid core wood doors? Light hollow doors? All of this stuff matters since your landlord may require certain types of doors in your suite. Most doors must conform to a certain look and standard that matches the rest of the doors in the building. These are simple decisions, but just make sure your contractor provides good quality doors that adhere to the building's and landlord's requirements.

Painting and wall base: What kind of paint are they giving you? How many coats? Is your building landlord okay with different paint colors inside your suite, even if they deviate from the standard dental office colors? *Also, ask your contractor if paint will be applied before or after cabinetry is installed.* If it is before, the contractor should touch up the suite after cabinets are installed since there will be areas that they've scuffed.

Flooring: Flooring is another suite feature that can really characterize your office. What types of floors are included in the bid? If it's wood, is it real wood or wood laminate? Are you getting a bid for carpet in the front office and back office? Know the plan beforehand.

Exclusions: Exclusions are often overlooked when perusing the bid. Usually, these fees will be excluded: *Any taxes, school fee, sewer fee, special assessment fees, or any surcharges from the city or county to which your project belongs.* Other items that can be excluded are *alarm systems, computer cables, TV cables, TV brackets, signs, blinds, curtains, cup holders, towel holders, and so on.* It all depends on what your contractor has specified. In short, make sure you know exactly what is included and what is not. It's very discouraging when you're moving along in your project and find that something you thought you paid for wasn't included.

3. Choose a contractor who has built at least ten offices. A ton of contractors are out there ready to build your dream office. To a certain extent, it's a matter of following the construction plan and hammering away with the vision that has been laid out on the design blueprints. But it's not that simple. Since this is likely your first time doing this, it would be good to know that your contractor has done this a bunch of times before. All of my contractors have built over fifty offices, and this put me at ease knowing that I didn't need to know everything. There is an element of trust in this whole equation that you need to be comfortable with. My recommendation is that you choose someone with experience who knows the potential problems, specifically with building out dental offices. These contractors already know the average treatment room size or the ideal location to mount an x-ray unit. A good mix of contractor experience infused with your vision of a world-class office is a winning combination.

4. Set an exact finish date and agree on a per-day fee if it has not been completed. Now this is a BIG one! Every contractor is going to give you the best, most optimistic timeline when it comes to finishing up your office. You need to have them put their money where their mouth is! Don't be afraid to hold them to their timeline. I've found that three months to complete an office is a reasonable timeline. This does not include the time it takes to get the permits to start building or the Temporary Certificate of Occupancy. Your three-month timeline should begin when construction begins. Make sure you mark this date on your iPhone, or Smartphone. If your builder goes over the end date, then make him or her pay on a per day basis. I think a penalty of $200 per day for any days over the agreed-upon time of completion is more than fair. Remember, time equals money. You can't afford to be delayed by even a day because every day you don't see patients is one more day you aren't making money to pay the rent, pay your bills and, most importantly, pay yourself.

5. Discuss a telephone, audio, and computer plan. Are phone and audio components listed in your contract? Many times these items will not be in the contract. In this case, you will have to find another contractor to complete this part. Consider these important components when you begin construction since your phone, audio, and computer subcontractor need to coordinate placement of these items. How many phone lines do you want?

Where will your phones be located? Where will you put your computers: behind the patient chairs, toward the side, or both? How many speakers are in your suite? For these reasons, the subcontractor that installs these items should also be familiar with your design plans. In addition, your general contractor needs to know where the computer conduits will be installed in order to make the appropriate provisions when building out your suite. Computer conduits are one or two-inch piping that houses cat5e (computer cables) data cable lines to power your computers. This is all pretty simple stuff, but I am pointing it out so you can plan for these items during your build-out. If your general contractor already has a subcontractor on the team who handles all of this, schedule a meeting to discuss a good price. Also, remember that it's really convenient to get some other bids on this particular part of the build-out. Once again, work with someone who has experience in the build-out of dental offices.

PAYING YOUR CONTRACTOR

Paying your contractor is an important part of the whole scenario. First, let's review the basics of business and finance before we discuss paying your contractor. I've included this section because it's important to **know how much and when** you should pay your contractor. *Never pay a huge chunk of money up front; if the contractor requests that you do, then find another one.* Most contractors will be more than happy to work out a pay schedule, so make sure you negotiate one that is fair, and ensure it gives you some leverage.

Whether you are funding your build-out through a bank loan, a tenant improvement allowance, or through family members who want to invest in your office, you must manage the accounting. The best way to do this is to have a legal entity activated prior to paying anything out. Go to Legalzoom.com and get your legal entity (S corp or C corp, for example), and have a bank account opened up in that legal identity. Make payments from that account so that you know where the funds for your project are coming from. This will also help you maximize your deductions and losses when you file your taxes. Along with a bank account, get a business credit card under that legal entity's name so that you can keep transactions structured from the very beginning. Trust me. When the build-out begins, the money will be dispersed to your vendors and various subcontractors quicker then you think, so you must keep things in order here.

Payment Rule: *Always keep the bigger portion of money in your pocket as you move forward with your build-out.* If possible, hold the bulk of your money until the end of the build-out. The reason is that some contractors will get slow or lazy on the job if you pay them all they want up front. Therefore, it's best to pay them in installments as jobs are completed. It sounds like I'm being prudent, but you will see that it is the only way to do it. I have included a payment schedule below that shows you a sample payout sequence with specific markers showing when to pay your contractor.

PAYMENT SCHEDULE BASED ON A TOTAL BUILD-OUT COST OF $176,000:

- 5% on signing of contract ($8,800)
- 20% at start of construction ($35,200)
- 5% after framing and electrical wiring installation ($8,800)
- 30% after completion and inspection (*and* passing) of plumbing, electrical and framing ($52,800)
- 30% after cabinets and flooring installed ($52,800)
- 10% after final inspection ($17,600)

This is the same schedule or at least very similar to the ones that I have followed in all my build-outs. Notice how I kept about 40 percent of the total build-out cost until the very end of the build-out, which is roughly $70,000 sitting in my pocket or waiting to be paid out not one minute before the job is completed. Under these circumstances, do you think the contractor has motivation for finishing the job? You bet they do, and you always want to keep that financial leverage on your side during a build-out.

You've come a long way! You've learned what elements to use in creating an extraordinary office with a world-class presence. You've also learned how to use a formula that can help you achieve a high level of predictability during your build-out. You know how to hire a contractor and how to evaluate competing construction bids. Now, it's time to build! Say *what*? Where do you place the first nail?

Chapter 6

LET'S BUILD!

Build it and they will come,
and come in droves I say!

Now that you've chosen a contractor you're comfortable with, you are ready to begin construction. Below is a detailed timeline to help you successfully complete your dream office build-out from start to finish. Using this timeline will also help you manage your time and track the progress of your contractor. I've divided it into increments so that the steps are easy to follow and allow you to plan ahead. Every construction sequence is always somewhat different, but there is also a common thread in every project, which is what I have presented here. I've included some of my own checklist items that you'll need to check off as you move forward. On the right, next to each action, fill in a realistic timeline to keep yourself on track.

The actions that are in one box are the ones that you can be doing simultaneously.

Action	Timeline
☐ Find a location	
☐ Negotiate lease with landlord	
☐ Plan office spacing and design	
☐ Submit plan to various contractors for bids ☐ Submit design to landlord for approval and discuss any other questions or concerns	
☐ Select a contractor and sign contract ☐ Submit final office design to the city for approval	
☐ Obtain Temporary Certificate of Occupancy (TCO) from city ☐ Begin construction!	
☐ Obtain rough build-out/ structural approval by city (framing, slab, space allocations, etc.)	
☐ Obtain electrical approval from city	
☐ Obtain plumbing and mechanical approvals from city	
☐ Paint office	
☐ Install cabinetry	
☐ Lay flooring elements	
☐ Install dental equipment	
☐ Retouch paint as needed	
☐ Install carpeting	

Action	Timeline
☐ Obtain final inspections from city to be granted final building occupancy	
☐ Install computer elements, wall, and ceiling mounts	
☐ Install phone system	
☐ Set up surround sound audio system	
☐ Negotiate credit card and set up and install terminal	
☐ Upload dental software systems and provide training for all employees	
☐ Buff, polish, and seal the floors	
☐ Begin interviewing new staff for hire	
☐ Perform a walk-through with mock patients, including family and friends	

Below you'll find a summary of everything in the timeline above. Some of it might seem redundant since we've just reviewed it, but I really want to reinforce the sequence of actions so that when you build your office, you don't get lost in the details.

Let's walk through it once more to make sure you've got it!

After choosing a location for your office, you should start interviewing three to five different contractors that meet the criteria that we emphasized earlier. During this time, you should also be looking for a resource to design your office. Remember the design can be accomplished either through the contractor that you find or another designer or architect that you acquired through your dental supply company, or even your landlord. After you have a space plan, inform the contractors that you've interviewed. Keeping key construction elements in mind, compare their bids and make your selection. Direct your contractor to city hall to get the necessary approvals to commence construction in your city. You may be required to pay some minor fees associated with the approval process.

Then, you'll need to oversee the rough build-out by visiting the site at least once or twice a week. This will ensure your contractor is framing your suite accordingly. During this phase of construction, it is very easy to make changes or adjustments. For example, if you decide that a wall or curve should not be there or should be more pronounced, now is the time to let your contractor know. An easy way to do this is to carry measuring tape with you to the site. Be familiar with the measurements of your new office, the treatment rooms, front desk area, and so forth. Know the level of inspection for each stage of the build-out process, and always ask your contractor for a timeline goal with regard to upcoming inspections. You might say something like this: "Now that we've finished the rough inspection with the city, when do you anticipate calling them for the electrical inspection?" This will alert them to the fact that you are keeping an eye on the progress and expect construction to continue to move along in a timely manner. Remember that delays mean fewer patients as the year progresses.

In the timeline above, I have the contractors paint the office first and then install the cabinetry to avoid any paint finding its way onto the cabinetry. Flooring should be done after the cabinets are in to prevent scuffing the floors. If you are following this sequence, have your contractor re-touch the paint after the cabinets have been installed *and* the flooring is in.

Finally, lay your carpet in the areas you designated and install your phone, audio, and computer systems. I recommend having two to three lines to start since you will be building your call volume after you open. Designate a reliable server as the home to all your software systems, and make sure you are backing it up either to a cloud storage service (online and accessible from anywhere) or to an external hard drive.

PITFALLS AND RED FLAGS

Building three offices has certainly exposed many pitfalls and red flags during construction, most of which were resolved. Watch for the following when you begin to build:

Ceiling space: Your ceiling is the T-Bar or drywall that you will look up at while standing. Above the T-Bar is the circuitry of the office. Make sure your contractors leave around three feet above the T-Bar for the ventilation system, the plumbing pipes, and the computer cables. In one of my offices, it was a tight squeeze up there because I wanted a ten-foot-high ceiling (ten feet from the floor to the T-bar ceiling tile); but above the T-bar there wasn't enough room as we needed a certain amount of room to slant the plumbing lines to comply with the city guidelines. We settled on nine-foot, six-inch ceilings, and it worked out.

Sink: Buy sinks that are durable for patient use and avoid the trendy sinks that tend to leak with multiple uses.

Flooring: Before you lay any flooring in your suite, inspect and make sure that all areas are level and smoothly sanded down, watching for cracks in the cement. Uneven or wavy pavement or cracks in the pavement can translate into separation in your flooring whether it's PVC tile or laminate wood flooring.

Electrical outlets: Do regular walk-throughs of your office space as they start to build, and envision where your technology and powered units will be located. You should have plenty of electrical outlets in your sterilization areas, treatment rooms, and even reception area as these are all areas that will require some kind of powered equipment.

Reinforcements: Know where you want to mount TV screens, computer monitors, x-ray units, and even artwork. The wall where you will be mounting these items must have some extra support, referred to as *backing*. Point out these areas to your contractor so that he or she can place some wood reinforcements in the correct areas.

Lighting: If you have niches, place some lighting on the top of the arch; it's a nice touch. Also, always make sure you have enough overhead light in your treatment rooms because the last thing you want is a dark treatment room due to poor planning.

Air flow: If you have a suite with a lot of windows (and I hope you do), then you'll need to know the air flow paths since temperature changes in these areas are more drastic. Have your contractor balance the air in the suite accordingly so that you get more heat to the cooler areas and cooler air to the hotter ones. You don't want your patients sweating up a storm as you work on them. A great tip here is to have two control units for the A/C, one for the reception area, and one for the back office. In one of my offices, we have one control for the entire office, so the front office cools a lot faster than the back office. Sometimes this can turn into a comfort inconvenience issue. For this reason, it's worth having two controls.

Measurements, cabinetry, and chalking: This is an area where you can run into some trouble if you don't meticulously plan for adequate spacing and room size. This is a big reason why I recommend hiring a contractor who has constructed at least ten offices; experienced contractors know how big rooms should be. Always go with comfortable-sized rooms because they are less intimidating.

The distance from the front entrance to the edge of the reception area front desk should be at least nine to ten feet. A wide-open entrance provides a grand suite ambience. Similarly, treatment rooms should be no smaller than eight feet wide, including no side cabinetry. Personally, I like rooms that are nine to ten feet wide. If you make all the rooms a similar size, your office will look more uniform. Don't make your sterilization and lab areas too small as these will be high-traffic areas for your staff, especially as your business grows.

Make sure your front desk and cabinetry space is large enough for the maximum number of reception area staff you expect to have. If, for example, you've chosen a small front desk where three staff members sit, the area will look crammed and it will probably decrease productivity.

While your contractor drafts up designs for your cabinetry and front desk, it's important that you measure your equipment and computer technology to determine the counter space you'll need. You'll want to have enough free space so that your counters don't look crammed or cluttered.

Countertops in my office are anywhere from forty to forty-eight inches wide, depending on where they are. Avoid some pitfalls with measurements and space planning by having your contractor and cabinet person come out and chalk up the floor where the cabinetry and desk will be located, along with their actual projected sizes. Just make sure you tell them you want this done before anything is delivered. I even had my equipment vendor come out and chalk up the sizes of the chairs that I ordered so that we could see what things looked like in the rooms even before the framing began. This is very helpful since you can actually see the chairs on the floor in white chalk, giving you an accurate mental picture. Small and important requests such as these will save you a lot of guesswork and modifications. In addition, if you need to make modifications, you'll have time to make them before anything is delivered.

CONGRATS!

By now, you should have a clear build-out sequence in mind with a rough timeline for seeing the project through to completion and paying your contractor accordingly. You now know what to focus on when building your office and how to oversee the entire project. If you keep the pitfalls of construction in mind, you'll be able to navigate your practice to the finish line with success and a greater deal of predictability. Now, it's time to build your practice, market your business, and add tremendous value to your community through your services and business practices. To do this, you'll need to build a team that shares your vision.

Chapter 7

CREATING YOUR DREAM TEAM

*"Coming together is a beginning. Keeping together is progress.
Working together is success." ~Henry Ford*

You can be the most talented dentist out there with the most restorative, orthodontic, and periodontal knowledge and expertise. You can flaunt your Super-Dentist ways and attend seminars every other week, but you are only as good as your team. When we realize that it's our teams that create the offices we build and without them we are just solo practitioners, a new way of service can begin. Imagine having to open your office every day. Imagine being the first one in the office, setting up before anyone else came in, and being the last one to leave, cleaning up after everyone left. This is not how the owner should be running any business. I know dentists who take home claims they need to bill out every week or month. You should trust your team to do that for you! This reminds me of a fitting quote by Brendon Burchard(author of The Charge) that puts it into perspective: "Don't let your small business make you small-minded." You're not only the dentist, but also the CEO. Act like one! Not like a pompous CEO, but one who understands that to be successful, you must first think big and then *inspire others on your team to do the same.* In this chapter, we will review the basic tenets for creating your dream team.

Yes, dentistry is important, but the right team can make you look like a superstar. Wouldn't you feel better going to work knowing that you are respected and well-liked? In your dental practice, you are the CEO, but you're also working with the employees. Forget everything the other business books are telling you and remember that your team needs to *like* you and *respect* you. If you have just one attribute here but not there, you have only half the influence. Let me explain.

We live in a *like-me* world. Take Facebook's *"Like"* button, for example. Almost a billion people are encouraged to be "Liked" by their peers and give "Likes" to people, music, causes, and businesses. I can assure you that, in your office, it's no different. This is a new day, a day in which companies spend a good amount of energy and strategy figuring out ways their employees can be more satisfied, challenged, and productive—all at the same time. So, how do you earn respect and garner esteem? *They will respect you if you encourage excellence and success in them, and they will like you if you treat them with respect at the same time.* Read that again! If you remember nothing else in this chapter, remember that. Encourage excellence and success in every task they perform. Tell them they did it right, and show them how to do it right if they did it wrong. Tell them in a way you yourself would want to be told. The key is to interact with your staff respectfully. But where does it all start?

Notice that this section is titled *"Creating* Your Dream Team" and not *"Hiring* Your Dream Team." Dentistry is a unique field in and of itself. You undergo eight to ten years of extensive training(undergrad, dental school, residency/specialty) and then you enter the profession prepared to practice four-handed dentistry. What do you find instead? That four-handed dentistry is just a myth! That is, until you learn the art of hiring and training superstars. No other profession exists where you spend so many years training in the sciences to be paired with an assistant who has completed a basic dental assisting program or, better yet, one who has been in the field for ten years and has picked up all the bad habits from other offices. Attorneys have well-trained paralegals; physicians have physician's assistants and nurses. But dentists have the most poorly trained staff, and it's not getting any better. Just watch the movie *Waiting for "Superman"* and see how our future workforce is being trained and the results of our education system across America. Don't get me wrong; there are some great schools and educational institutions out there, but most of them are really struggling with discipline, structure, and effective guidance from instructors. You won't always find excellence at a school, but you can create it in your office. What does all this mean to us dentists? We've got to train our team! *It's not the school that's great; it's usually the students who have the ability to be great. We must harness that potential and integrate it effectively into our practice and vision.*

If you don't have the patience to train or the ability to provide mentorship and guidance to the people on your team, you will not be successful. It is more important now than ever before to have an outstanding team because your patients want the very best. And if you are charging top dollar for quality care, you'd better have the best team in town.

20 SECRETS FOR CREATING YOUR DREAM TEAM

1. **Write an office manual specifically for your office.** Don't give your team a generic manual that you copied from another office. Write one for your office by using a template and adding your own elements. Treat this task as a priority as your staff needs to know exactly what you expect from them on a daily basis. Make sure you have one for the front office staff as well as the back office team. A brand new member of our team, for example, should know exactly what he or she needs to do when writing a lab slip. It usually takes a new member of our team about a month to settle in. A comprehensive training system, just like the one I am describing, will ensure your new employee makes a smooth transition into his or her new roles and responsibilities. Does your team know what constitutes acceptable workplace attire? Do they know which holidays are paid days? Are they comfortable escorting patients from the reception area to the dental chair?

Do they know what to tell patients when they are reviewing a treatment plan? Have they memorized the fees? Are they familiar with your dental services and treatments, and are they able to provide accurate descriptions of these services and explain to patients what treatments are available? You should have clear and concise systems and answers for all of these questions. Thus, the goal of the office manual is to provide a structure and *system* for your team to follow.

Encourage creativity, not for systematic tasks such as these, but in creative areas of the business, such as patient satisfaction, interaction, and even team marketing. As far as systems and protocol, be clear, have a system, and *teach* according to that system. There are some dentists that have office manuals, yet they don't teach from them. When your staff asks you a question, refer to the manual and say, *"According to the manual, this is what should be done."* This way, your team knows that what is in that manual is what's important, and it becomes a *resource for answers* they can refer to. If you want to know more about creating effective systems and protocol, read the book *E-Myth Revisited*; it has changed the way I run my office. Every dentist should get this book and start implementing what's in it immediately, along with what's in this book. Your goal should be to have a system and set of sequences for your staff to follow, an easy-to-follow system that takes them from point A to point Z.

WHAT TO INCLUDE IN YOUR OFFICE MANUAL:

- How to answer phone calls effectively so that patients make appointments
- Rules for scheduling patients for each doctor
- A written fee schedule itemizing fees broken down by actual practice fees and UCR fees
- How to write up a lab slip
- How to confirm appointments
- How to gather necessary patient data

- How to set up a follow-up plan for patients
- How dental assistants should set up for dental procedures
- Pictures of setups for procedures specific to the treatment
- Daily routines for dental assistants and front office staff
- Dental assistant and front office staff responsibilities
- How to escort patients from the reception area to the dental chair
- Rules of ordering supplies
- The sterilization process
- Step-by-step guide to calculating insurance benefits
- Templates for working with insurance companies and obtaining benefits information
- Daily office close-out procedures
- Daily financial close-out procedures

Explicit and thorough communication with regard to job duties is the key to success with your team. Create a job-specific manual for each position in your office, and encourage staff members to read it and update it periodically.

2. Look online. Craigslist.com, dentalworkers.com, dentaljobs.com, and monster.com are just a few of the online job search portals that our office has used. We've also found qualified candidates straight from dental assisting schools. So, my suggestion is to establish contact with your local dental assisting school, and ask if they can recommend any students for an externship. As far as online sites, I have always felt that monster.com is highly overpriced for our particular industry with a poor selection of candidates from search terms such as *dental assistant* or *office manager*. Most of our great employees were found either through craigslist.com or through our local dental assisting programs.

3. Conduct at least three paid working interviews. When you first meet someone interviewing for a position in your office, it's always a very surface-level meeting. It takes a few interviews to really get a grasp of that person's intentions. Set the tone early on with the kind of a business you operate and your vision for your practice. Pay them a small hourly fee for their working interview if the situation calls for it. We pay all of our working interviews $10 per hour. Now, I know this is way above minimum wage and also way below what some great assistants and front office staff are truly worth, but it's fair for an assistant that doesn't know how your office runs. By paying them at the outset, you are sending a message to them that you are giving them the benefit of the doubt, and now they have to provide the proof via performance. Ninety-five percent of the time, after a working interview, candidates usually want to work with our company, leaving it for us to decide whether we want him or her on our team. When you interview, present your best company vision so you can make sure you *choose* the best.

4. Hire new, inexperienced, but highly motivated and professional candidates. I'd take this combo any day over a difficult employee with a ton of experience. I like hiring employees at a competitive hourly rate, watching them grow and improve in their job performance, and then increasing their pay. For me, this is more rewarding than hiring someone at the peak of his or her hourly position. If, however, you get someone with reasonable experience and an amazing mind-set, and this person has the potential to be the face of your company, don't turn him or her away. With that being said, I encourage you to hire new, inexperienced, but highly motivated and professional people. I have employees in my offices that have been with me for over six years full-time! Unfortunately, in our industry, this is rare. But it doesn't have to be. After all, you are the one inspiring, motivating, and leading your team on a daily basis! Think about it. Why would an employee go somewhere else when working for you is so rewarding and satisfying? *When people feel better about where they are and who they are with, they perform better.*

5. Establish an online team setup. This is tremendously important! Online communication with all of your assistants and front office team is essential. Most offices don't have personal e-mail addresses for their staff. To remedy this situation, assign everyone an office e-mail address. You can easily do this through the variety of web hosting services out there. One of these is Godaddy.com. *Get everyone a company e-mail account.* It's inexpensive and sets the tone for more professional communication. In our practices, we have an efax account that forwards faxes in .pdf format to our front office staff. For instance, if you get a fax from an insurance company, it's automatically forwarded to the person who handles insurance-related tasks. For us, that includes everyone in the reception area; for you, it might be just one of two people. You can also display a company calendar to keep your staff up to date on important meetings within the office. The take-away message here is that it's all organized, electronically documented, and easy to find. Waste less time and save trees in the process; it's a win-win setup.

6. **Change how you look at them.** This next insight is inspired by Dr. Wayne Dyer, an author and speaker. Dr. Dyer is often quoted as saying, "If you change the way you look at things, the things you look at change." This couldn't be a truer statement for your team! Look at them with the potential, hope, and conviction that they will succeed in your practice. Let them know that you are here to help them succeed. Expect the best from them, and watch them meet or exceed your expectations. Most dentists get frustrated too quickly with their team. I challenge you to use this way of leading your team. Try it, and see the results it brings you. *Remember, your employees will support what they create.* See them as creators in your practice: creators of good will, creators of study models, lab slips, and even creators of scheduling. Give them this higher-tier control, and watch them improve. Always keep in mind, people grow towards what is expected of them. Expect greatness.

7. **Realize that you are also there to *inspire* your team.** It's never always just about the business. They need to know that you care and have their best interest at heart. You need to make your team feel good, and I mean *really* good about themselves and their self-image. Steve Wynn, the self-made billionaire and founder of modern-day Vegas and the visionary behind the Encore, Bellagio and Wynn resorts, was speaking at Tony Robbins' business mastery event in Las Vegas. He told the audience that the number one thing you can do for your staff is to make them feel exceptional about what they do every chance you get. If you could tie their self-image and sense of worth to something great they did at work and then recognize them for this, you will forever have a loyal team member. We recently began doing this in our offices by taking the positive online

reviews written by our patients and displaying them in our staff lounge. Some of the reviews even include names of the dental assistants, which is a bonus. Staff members love reading about the good job they did or how much a patient likes seeing them. This is just one way in which we have applied Steve Wynn's philosophy of connecting your staff's self-image or self-worth to something great they did at work; the most powerful action here is acknowledging it through sharing those reviews with everyone else in the staff lounge.

Something more immediate yet often overlooked is to comment on something that your staff members did *right* with a patient. It doesn't have to be a big deal; it can be as small as how they said that patient's name or the energy they shared with patients during an appointment. How about the story they shared with that patient during their appointment? One of my assistants once told me she grew up going to military school on the weekends and that she'd have to run eight miles every weekend at 6 a.m.! I found this so interesting and was inspired myself from the discipline involved in doing this. Whenever we spoke of fitness with our patients during casual conversation, I would always use my assistant's story as inspiration. Not only are the patients wowed by this, but my assistant (who stood silently nearby) appreciated that I revered her story enough to share it with our patients.

8. Be a professional boss. Whether you like it or not, as an owner, your staff and those you employ look to you to lead. *Remember that there is no greater leader than the one who has been chosen to lead.* All this means is that by being a business owner, you have been designated as leader, and your staff *automatically* assigns that role to you. Remember this: you set the standard, and if you are always missing the mark and incompetent, you can't expect your team to be any different. Lead with integrity, professionalism, and understanding. We are in a business of making people feel comfortable and changing their lives through great dental care and wellness. Don't talk about your drunken nights out with the buddies or how you didn't feel like coming to work today. Be professional about the way you present yourself. *Your profession is a reflection of your professionalism.*

9. Have specific duties outlined for everyone in your practice. This is critical to the success of every person on your team. If staff members are uncertain about their job duties, they will stray from the task at hand and create work that they think is important. You want your team to be creators, but you should also give them a clear and concise framework in which to create. This involves assigning clear, written workday responsibilities. What you want to avoid is your assistants and office managers *creating protocol just because* they have none in a particular area.

10. Review and evaluate what you have outlined. Remember this, *what is reviewed is respected and upheld.* Your staff will respect whatever you *regularly* review. Let's say that I told my back office manager that we can order only $1,000 worth of dental supplies each month and that this was our budget. He or she would be fine with this at first, but if I didn't evaluate this regularly, he or she may not adhere to it. If you show them that you are evaluating the systems you are creating, they will respect the systems as well.

A great example is outlining a system for answering phone calls. In our offices, we have an outlined procedure for conversations with a new patient. But how do we evaluate this? We record conversations from certain promotions and play them back when we train our team. This can all be done via a cool online service called Kall8. You get an 800 number, tag it to your current promotion, and then have calls recorded when patients call in from that number. If you think your team knows how to work the phones, just listen to their calls; you may be surprised. Have your team review the calls during a meeting in a playful way so that everyone can improve their phone etiquette. If you want to know what message your office is sending to those that call, then listen to what your staff is saying on the phones. It's that plain and simple, phone etiquette must always be evaluated and improved!

11. Schedule 1½-hour monthly meetings with all of your team. When we started this, the connectivity within our team immediately went up. But don't let these meetings turn into a rant session; instead, infuse the spirit of where you want your company to go next. Your goal as a leader is to give your team something valuable at every meeting. Sometimes I will play a DVD on business management or personal development, and other times I will share some of the lessons that I have learned from a particularly good book and show them how to apply it to our business. Fifteen percent of the meeting should focus on identifying the troubled areas, 60 percent on finding solutions, and 25 percent on personal development within the company. The development portion could include effective time management techniques, how to gain more energy and vitality in your day, or—one of my favorites—how to enjoy better health. Your team will appreciate your adding value to *their* lives. Sometimes, I will devote 50 percent of my meeting to personal development alone.

So, what happens after the meetings? Immediately afterwards, the office manager should e-mail your entire team a bulleted list of items discussed and resolved during the meeting. This way, problems and solutions are documented and presented as goals to take action on immediately.

12. Show them how to make more money. It all comes down to consistently evaluating your team and having explicit outlines for all the duties that every assistant and front office team member has in your office. For example, we have our performance review sheet posted on a wall in the back office, and during our semi-annual reviews the doctors and office managers fill out these sheets and evaluate our team members based on those criteria. Since they know exactly what they are being evaluated on and receive feedback directly related to their job performance, this is the most reliable way to ensure your team members get the raises they deserve. We recently implemented a new incentive system in our practices. If the office reaches a certain financial goal for that month, everyone gets a fixed dollar amount. For instance, if we hit $80,000 in collections for the month, $2,000 is divided among our two assistants and two front office staff members. If there are two front office employees and two back office employees, each receives an additional $500 on his or her paycheck for that month! Get your team involved and post weekly updates on financial and new patient statistics; this will give them a financial goal to aim for. When you incentivize your team every month, they get more excited every day and feel that their goals are in close grasp, as opposed to incentivizing every 3 months, or half year.

13. Offer health care benefits after six months. Because most dentists don't offer health insurance benefits to their employees, this is an excellent perk. Your team contributes to the success of your company, so why not contribute to their health and well-being? Plus, it sends them the powerful message that you value your staff. Six months gives you time to assess your new team members' abilities and intentions and determine whether or not they'll commit long term. Offering health benefits after six months also gives you a reason to terminate those on your team who are not A-listers.

14. If they need dental work, do it for free. To me, this is a no-brainer. Just have one of your assistants clock out and assist the one getting treatment and vice versa. Lab fees are the only fees that we charge to our immediate employees. When you do the same procedures for them as you do for your patients, your employees will talk about that procedure to your to patients. This benefit is one of the biggest endorsements because it gives patients the comfort they need to actually get the treatment done, especially if they are on the fence. It also sends the message to your team that you really do value dental care for them and sincerely care about their well-being.

15. Have occasional office dinners. It's important to develop and nurture camaraderie on your team, and one way to do that is by scheduling occasional get-togethers outside of work. Time spent together outside the office gives team members the opportunity to bond. Those who see their professional future with you will enjoy the positivity that results from team activities. Employees feel special when they know that you care enough to involve everyone on the team. Another idea is to get your team members involved as volunteers. One of our doctors is involved with local dental charities and encourages everyone else to get involved, too. I joined him on one trip and loved it. Your team will appreciate that you value unity and camaraderie.

16. Buy lunch when you can. Buying lunch for your staff is a simple gesture, and it's inexpensive. Google provides free food for all their employees. Quite a few companies have begun giving comfort benefits, such as food, healthy snacks, and relaxation hours to their employees. As it may be tough to take a relaxation break when you have five patients waiting to be seen, you can still provide comfort perks such as buying lunch on certain days of the week.

17. Hire slowly and fire quickly. Read this three times because you will fail at it at least once! I have and sometimes still do. We are all hopeful entrepreneurs who want the best for our staff, but we also must be smart businessmen and women who remove the bad apples quickly. A sour employee who's been given *documented* chances to improve their performance but doesn't meet the standard after three months of phasing into the company should be terminated promptly. Meet with them to discuss problem areas and solutions and then e-mail them what you discussed and agreed upon in the meeting. Make sure you request that the employee reply to your e-mail so that you have a documented acknowledgment of your expectations. E-mail is an effective way of doing this as it's informal and less threatening. Although you are not officially writing them up, the terms agreed upon during the meeting have been documented.

18. Refresh your team. By *refresh* I mean keeping your team fresh with new energy. Now, I don't suggest you fire everyone on your team to get that new energy, but I am not opposed to taking those actions either, if need be. What this essentially means is that if you are creating a superstar team with members who want to be around year after year, they may start to feel as if they are owed something since they have *been there* for so long. I don't support this type of thinking! Your employees should never assume they can get better treatment elsewhere or get away with poor performance simply because they've been there for a while. Rather, they need to know and be reminded occasionally that good **performance and service are expected; it is a given.** *They must realize that their time in your office is only equal to their current efforts and level of performance.* Simply stated, perform well today and be valued because you've been here for so long. Start performing poorly, and it won't matter that you've been here for so long. I don't pay for poor performance and longevity, and neither should you. If you notice poor performance in your team members and you've sat down with them and addressed your concerns but it never gets resolved, then it's time to fire quickly and refresh with a new member. Don't allow anyone to give your team a stale mentality. Refresh immediately! As much as I value building our team, I also see the importance of *refreshing.*

19. Read the book *E-Myth Revisited* by Michael Gerber. I mentioned this book earlier, but I can't emphasize enough the value and importance of its message. It is absolutely critical for the success of small business owners such as dentists. A great read for every business owner, this book explains how to set up the systems and protocols in your office to automatize high performance, and not struggle to squeeze it out of your team.

20. Read *The Ultimate Sales Machine* by Chet Holmes. This book delves into the psychology of education-based marketing. Translated into dental practice terms, it focuses on adding value to your patients before you can expect anything in return from them. Educate your patients, and they will come to you for answers and treatment. Patient education has taken over the marketplace. Using this approach enables you to find and keep the best patients who respect what you do and trust your intentions. Talk about the simple things that many dentists overlook! Educate them on the importance of teeth, not just filling cavities; show them the **data** that suggest that one's lifestyle, digestion, and self-esteem can improve due to great oral care. *Educate them on their well-being then show them how their teeth and oral health tie into that education.* Chet Holmes does a superior job, and his book is an ultra-valuable read for any dentist practicing today.

Chapter 8

MASTERING THE PHONES

*The only thing that stands between you and
your patients is your gatekeeper.*

Why will some people make an appointment and come into your office while others just call and then don't come in? What's the real influence behind this difference? Without a doubt, its all about the way your front office staff answers the phones! Telephone etiquette can really make or break your business. That's right! All of your years of schooling are worthless because the person answering the phone is the *gatekeeper* for your practice. He or she will be the most important human element between a new patient scheduling with you or hanging up and calling the dentist down the street.

I have always placed a high value on the way we handle phone calls. In fact, new hires are forbidden from even answering a single phone call until they know *exactly* what to say. If we are running a promotion, they must know exactly what that promotion is all about, what's included, what's not, and how the procedure works. I want to make sure the people answering our phones are not just good, but phenomenal. You should aim for this as well. The patient on the other end should hang up the phone and think,

Wow, she was amazing. I got much more than I thought I would. Giving them *much more* then they thought they'd get is the first step to adding value. Give your callers that level of presence and undivided attention, information, and enthusiasm on the phone so they not only know, but *feel* you are different. Now, not every staff member will be able to accomplish this, but it is a skill that can be taught, and you must strive for that level of performance on the phones.

Below are the keys to mastering the phones for your front office team. Train your team to integrate these 10 insights and you're patients will keep calling and also scheduling!

10 INSIGHTS TO MASTERING THE PHONES

1. **Endorse:** We have a few doctors that work in our practices. When the team schedules an appointment for a new patient for a particular doctor, they are also instructed to endorse that doctor. The concept of endorsing goes a long way. When someone tells a patient that Dr. Ganatra really is great and easy to talk to, don't you think it comforts your patient? Of course it does! If you go into the Apple store, does the Apple expert simply show you the different products and tell you to choose? No way! The expert points out the differences between the MacBooks and the desktop computers. You rely on their expertise when making your decision. Successful businesses, like Apple, endorse their products, and so should you. We have treated many of our team members' family and friends, and it's really gratifying to hear them tell the patient, "Yeah, Dr. SuperDentist is awesome and my family really likes him as well. I'm sure you'll love him." Train your team to endorse *you.* Never schedule an appointment by saying you are seeing so and so, and your appointment time is at this time. Add an endorsement; it reassures the patients and puts them at ease before they even step foot in the office.

2. **Be present:** The worst conversations are those you have with people who are not *there*! If your front office manager is answering phones and distracted about a treatment plan she has to finish, patients will sense that lack of presence. Value attentiveness and make it a part of your customer service training. Documenting important patient information requires you and your staff members' undivided attention, so be 100 percent present when you interact with your patients on a phone call. When you do this, you are telling them that their questions and concerns are your priority.

3. **Engage:** Don't allow your team members to be just another person answering the phones. Encourage them to ask patients questions about their life and their day. Constantly aim to connect with them. The best way to capture someone's attention and interest is to ask them questions and let them talk. *Listen* to what they say, but never let the patient have control of the conversation. By knowing and using the strategies to keep them engaged, you and your staff will always be in control of the conversation. For example, if a patient calls and says, "I really need a root canal on one of my teeth. When can you get me in for that?" An immediate response might be to schedule that patient for a root canal, but now the entire conversation is about scheduling for a root canal or emergency exam consult with a chance of endo. On the flip side, if your staff takes control of the conversation, that same patient can be taken care of by asking the right questions:

> **Receptionist:** What makes you think you need a root canal?
> **Patient:** I have a big cavity.
> **Receptionist:** Is it giving you a lot of pain? How about pain to hot/cold?
> **Patient:** It only hurts when I chew, but I can see that one of my fillings came out.
> **Receptionist:** I'm sorry to hear that. It's definitely not a good sign when your filling comes out; let's get you in immediately.

This is an example of engaging in and controlling the conversation and assessing the patient's needs. I could go on and on here, but make sure your front office staff is in control of the conversation and engaging with that patient appropriately by asking the right questions and then getting detailed answers to those questions as exemplified above.

4. **Express cheer:** Remember a time you called someone and they answered the phone with enthusiastic and happy tone of voice? Didn't that just set the tone for the entire conversation? It probably also raised your entire energy level during that conversation. Tone is contagious. Thirty-three percent of all communication comes from your tone of voice and only seven to eleven percent from the verbal content. So, if nearly half of what you are saying comes from how you are saying it, then how you say something can mean the difference between a patient scheduling with you or not. You don't have to overdo it when you answer, but keep an upbeat tempo, and whoever is calling you on the other end will notice it. Our front office team gets complimented all the time for being *too happy*. I hear them answer the phones, and I understand why people may think that, but they work hard at having that level of energy on the phones. It's important, and it feels great when others compliment them because I know they deserve it.

5. **Suggest an appointment time:** When I train a group of new front office staff on what to say during a phone call, this one is almost always overlooked. The staff assumes patients will ask to schedule an appointment. While this may be true some of the time, you must train your staff to *suggest* appointment times. You will book so many more appointments if you consistently suggest appointment times. Understand the distinction: don't ask them to schedule; rather, suggest an appointment. "We have a three o'clock appointment available for you with Dr. SuperDentist," for example. When you suggest a time, you automatically get them into the mind-set of thinking they have to schedule. Asking them, on the other hand, gives them an opportunity to think of all the reasons they can't schedule an appointment at this time. I understand that if people are set in their decision, then they simply won't schedule one. But don't you want your best psychology working for you rather than against you?

6. **Collect information:** While we emphasized the importance of controlling the conversation, your staff should be using patients' answers to document and build a patient history for their appointment. This includes insurance benefits, last dental visit, any pain they're experiencing, and a clear goal for their appointment that day. Establishing a goal is important because every patient calling your office will have one in mind and, during their visit with you, you'll want to ensure that their goal is accomplished. For instance, a patient's goal may be to come in, get his or her teeth cleaned, and have the front tooth looked at. If your staff records this information in the patient's chart, you'll know in advance your patient's chief concern.

7. **Never place them on hold:** This doesn't mean you should never place a phone call on hold. I know there are times when you'll have no other choice but to place a patient on hold. The key is knowing *when* to place patients on hold. In many offices, the person answering the phone will say, "Hello, Dr. Johnson's office. Can you hold, please?" This is the worst thing you can do. If you must place a patient on hold, do it after you acknowledge his or her reason for calling. Acknowledge, connect, and *then* place them on hold, if you must. When you acknowledge their reason for calling you're telling them that their reason for calling is more important than anything else happening in your office. Realistically, most patients will tell you why they are calling within a minute as long as you ask the right questions. This is an important minute; use it to connect, and then place them on hold if you have to.

8. **Confirm:** Be selective with your use of the words *confirming* and *reminding*. They are totally different. The rule is to confirm appointments immediately after scheduling, and remind them of this appointment when you call or e-mail them a day or two before the appointment. In other words, at the end of the phone call, tell them that the appointment is confirmed and that they will get a reminder call a day or two before. Most offices tell patients they will call them to confirm a day or two before the appointment time, but this *confirmation* gives your patients the opportunity to slide out of that appointment slot. Let them know they are confirmed after they have been scheduled and that, as a courtesy, you will call them a day before to remind them.

9. **Start and finish strong:** The way you begin a conversation is just as important as the way you end it; every phone conversation should leave the patient with a positive impression of you and your staff. We've covered ways to answer a call, but what happens when the conversation with a patient comes to an end? Before you or your staff members end a call, summarize the important details of the call for the patient, and express a cheerful anticipation of their appointment. Patients will hang up with all their questions answered and concerns addressed; they should be as eager for their appointment as you are to greet them when they come in. When they hang up, they should feel a refreshing sense of excellent customer service from the phone call they just had with your team.

10. **Forward the phones:** Make sure you forward the phones to someone in your office that can answer them after-hours. In our offices, we have office cell phones that one or two office members keep so that if we do get an emergency message, they can notify us of any call backs immediately. I don't use an after-hours service. I don't believe in sending an important call to a generic service that gets all types of calls. Don't be afraid to be different. Patients appreciate it when they can call your office and it actually goes to someone they know. Don't get me wrong; we don't always answer phone calls on Sundays, but if someone in pain leaves an important message, we'll get that message within hours. Stay connected and be available. Nine times out of ten, you'll return the call and prescribe something that will keep them comfortable through the weekend.

These ten insights can help your team master the art of answering phones! As you can see, these are not the same strategies we'd use to speak to our peers; they are specifically tailored to represent you and your practice in the best, most professional way possible.

Chapter 9

THE THREE STAGES

*First they know of you, then they come, and then they
send others to experience what they know of you.*

W OW! You've found a location, designed and built an office
you've always envisioned, groomed yourself into a leader, and
learned the strategies for building your dental dream team.
You've even trained your front office team to master the phones. Now, you
need some patients! You want your practice to attract the type of dentistry
and patient flow to match your brand, right? Where do we start, and how
do we approach this aspect of dental marketing?

When I started to grow my offices and watched patients fill our chairs
and keep returning for more, I noticed a trend in marketing, treatment
planning, and recalling. This repetitive trend of business growth was evi-
dent in all my practices. I formulated that growth and development into a
system that *harnesses the entire mind-set of growing a practice.*

In any office, there are three stages of growth, which can be summed
up using this simple acronym: ATR. Each letter represents a specific stage
of growth in your practice: Attraction, Treatment planning, and Return.

In fact, The ATR System is all you really need to know to grow your practice.

Ultimately, it's a success mind-set with a proven framework that will rapidly grow your office and increase your revenue.

Now, within the ATR System are a myriad of techniques that define each stage. Attraction, treatment planning, and return are all you need to experience explosive growth, and your marketing should reflect each stage. To market effectively, you *must* guide your patients through these three stages. Your marketing efforts will *attract* your patients and send them to your office; then, you'll plan out their treatment and, finally, they'll *return* for more services and treatment. At each stage, you'll consistently market your services to your patients. Most dentists miss this great opportunity; they don't understand the *value* meaning of marketing.

SUPERCHARGE YOUR MARKETING

Marketing is a BIG word, and it means so much to so many businesses. You hear it everywhere: You're so *marketable*. You need to *market*. How can we *market* this better? Who does your *marketing*? Now that's great *marketing*. We've all heard about marketing and advertising, and we learn more and more about its trends as businesses become globalized in a world of instant connectivity.

We could write a whole book on this one word alone! What is the essence of effective marketing? Try to look at marketing from a different perspective. All effective marketing should revolve around one concept. And using this concept, you have the potential to produce the most dynamic and lucrative marketing campaigns. Do you want to know what it is?

All effective marketing should aim to do just one thing: add massive value to your patients.

It's that simple.

MARKETING = CONSISTENTLY ADDING MASSIVE VALUE

You should aim to add massive value to the lives of your patients because they were exposed to you and your office. No one wants more mail, and no one wants yet another e-mail about your new promotion. Patients don't care about the newest laser in your office. They do, however, want to know **how it will be valuable to them.**

Add massive value to your patients by giving them MORE than they expect, and you will grow your practice beyond your dreams.

You should be adding massive value to your patients' lives in all three stages of the ATR System. Most dentists assume that once they attract new patients, the rest will take care of itself. You'll lose the game if you think that. Remember, attraction is only a third of the ATR System. The real magic begins after they make an appointment and come into your office.

What does marketing *really* mean?

To *attract* my patients, I need to add **massive value** to their lives by treatment planning them so that they are educated and motivated about improving their oral health. They *return* to my office because they get **massive value** from me and my team as we take care of them, educate them, and inspire them in ways they cannot get outside of our office.

All we did here was substitute the concept of **marketing** with **massive value.** Do this in all three stages of the ATR System. If you implemented this strategy in your office, you would always be busy with an unlimited flow of patients. In turn, they would refer others. I say this with full conviction since I have repeatedly done this in my offices.

Now that you really understand the success triad of the ATR System, let's turn our focus to the very first stage.

Chapter 10

ATTRACTION

The secret of attraction resides in your vision; you must start with the end in mind and then work backward. Become that practice that your patients would be drawn to, and then carve out the trail to your office.

A ttraction is the first stage of the ATR System. You can't run a business without patients. You have no business until your first patient walks into the office, and nothing matters until your patient is in the chair. Put another way, your education and expertise are worthless unless you have a butt in that chair! Recently a friend of mine, who is a dentist, told me about the most amazing course on porcelain veneers or smile design he had attended. He was under the impression that his participation in this course and his new knowledge would somehow attract patients and bring in tons of money. This is far from the truth; patients won't pay you until they truly feel you have THEIR best interest at heart *first*. And that is part of your marketing: to add massive value to their lives so that they feel comfortable and know that you genuinely care. This reminds me of my honeymoon. Let me share with you how attraction can work to bring you "pearls" of riches.

My wife and I traveled to French Polynesia for our honeymoon. It's an archipelago of 118 islands in the Pacific Ocean. We visited Bora Bora and Moorea, two of the most beautiful islands we had ever seen with crystal-clear, warm, turquoise-blue water, white sand, and lush greenery all around. I think it's an absolute paradise on earth. The water is so clear that you can see bright, colorful fish in the ocean just by looking over it!

A big industry in this region is black pearls. The sea life and oysters are so abundant that almost everyone comes back with a black pearl. Luckily for us, our travel agent had given us a "honeymoon package" deal, which included a free black pearl pendant. I didn't think it was a big deal until I landed and discovered the value of the market for black pearls. My wife, on the other hand, was really excited about getting her free black pearl pendant. All we had to do was show our voucher to the concierge in the resort who would then call the owner of the pearl shop. The owner of the pearl shop would pick us up from the hotel so that we could get our pearl. Hmm. They didn't just give you the pearl when you landed; you had to go pick it up from the shop.

So, a charismatic William picked us up in his Mercedes and pointed out the different stories and cultures of Moorea as he drove us to his shop. He also revealed that he makes a deal with most of the travel agents for travelers to get a voucher for a free black pearl. He didn't talk much about the pearls; he simply told us if we liked something else at the shop we could buy it, but if we didn't, that's fine as well as we were under no obligation to buy anything. *Interesting.* This guy was completely open and honest about his intentions and made it clear he wouldn't pressure us to buy anything. After forty-five minutes of circling the island and getting his perspective on the local history, we came to his shop.

It was a small shop with some beautiful pearls: silver, blue, and even striped. Our free pearl was ready for us in a small paper envelope, and it looked just as nice as the other ones in the shop. But, naturally, after we got the pearl, we looked around for a few minutes. William's family members, who worked at the shop, answered our questions and explained how the pearls were created. All of this they did with a genuine sincerity. It was then that my wife spotted this beautiful pearl necklace pendant encapsulated in sterling silver. We purchased it for around 20,000 Pacific francs (roughly $200). We both thought it looked gorgeous on her, and we were happy with the purchase. In the car on the way back to our resort, I jokingly said to William, "Great marketing, man!" He looked at me as if there was no secret and said, "Yes of course." He had focused on the first stage of growing his business exceptionally well: attraction.

William added value to our trip by one simple act: sharing funny and interesting stories about his native island during our drive to his shop. It's what *we* wanted to hear.

What do your patients want to hear from you? Are you talking to them about what *they* are interested in hearing or what *you feel* they should listen to? Where are your new patients, and how are you going to add massive value to their lives? You can't do this unless you first *have them in your office*. You must be diligent in establishing that sequence, that trail that leads them back to your practice. That is why we covered ten ways to master the phones. That phone call provides patients with an impression, a brand just by talking to the person who answered the phone.

A new patient calls your office and asks if they can come in for a free exam---> Sure, but **get them IN!**

Someone calls your office and asks if you see difficult kids---> Sure! Have them come in with their parents to see how difficult they are, but **get them IN!**

Someone calls your office and asks if you do braces----> The answer is you straighten teeth and, once they come in, you can decide what they need, so **get them IN!**

Someone calls and wants to meet the doctor before they schedule an appointment---> Sure! Be available and give them the tour of the office, but **get them IN!**

My point here is that if you don't get them in, *nothing* happens no matter how brilliant or knowledgeable you are. Your main focus—and you must relay this to your entire staff—is to get patients *inside* your office. Once patients are in your office, you and your team can work your magic on them and add some real value by educating and motivating them. But first, **get them IN!**

BRIGHT IDEAS

It was 2005, and I had started my first SoCal Smiles office in Rancho Santa Margarita, California. I was on the second floor along with three other dental offices down the hall. The entire second floor was all dentists: three general dentists and one pediatric dentist, all trying to restore teeth and improve dental care in the community, all new offices from scratch, and all on one floor. I worked as an associate two days a week fifty miles away and didn't have much of a loyal following there. In addition, since I was starting my office fifty miles from work, I figured that the patients who were big fans likely wouldn't follow me to my new location. The bottom line is that I had just opened up a new office and didn't have a single patient. Here I was in my gorgeous office plated with vibrant colors, state-of-the-art equipment, a truly paperless office with no files, and a welcoming and creative architectural design, but no new patients.

One day my office manager comes into my office and tells me that someone in the reception area wanted to see me for some "marketing stuff." At first I thought geez, *great. Another person telling me if I spend thousands a month with them, I'll get some new patients and if I don't, I should keep trying since it takes at least a few months anyway.* What other business can get away with saying, "If you don't get a response from what you are doing, keep doing it because eventually you *may* get a response." It was obvious that my confidence in conventional marketing was low, especially since I had just spent $10,000 on a direct mail campaign that returned absolutely no patients. Even so, I chose to stick to my inner game, which assured me that there is always a solution; you simply have to look away from the level of the problem. I walked to the reception area and greeted a representative from Bright Ideas Marketing. We went back into my office, and she told me their marketing plan for my office. Here is what she proposed:

Bright Ideas Marketing would sell a Zoom certificate in malls, colleges, trade shows, wedding conventions, and other places of mass gatherings. This certificate would include a comprehensive dental exam, x-rays, oral imaging, and one-hour Zoom teeth whitening. All of this for only $169, sold through a portable booth with a few "attractive" representatives from their company.

Those who purchase the gift certificate can visit any dentist they prefer as long as that dentist has a contract with Bright Ideas Marketing. Then, the dentist would perform the services covered by the certificate.

Okay, sounded good so far. But when I asked her when I would get the $169 for all the services that I performed (and here's the jaw-dropper), she told me I would get none of it and that Bright Ideas would keep the total amount from the sale of the certificate. WOW! I had to perform all those services and would get nothing in return. Well then, what would I really get out of this set-up? *I would get a new patient into my office.*

I was shocked by her proposal, but I still thought it was a genius idea. I was confident that if they came into my office and I was given the opportunity to connect with them, I could educate them and market my other services as well. When I asked her how many new patients I would get, she said it would vary anywhere from ten to forty. I was IN! Then I asked her why she came to my office. She said that she had asked all three of the other dentists on my floor and none of them thought it was good deal since they were not making any money for their services, especially since Zoom whitening kits were really expensive. They all thought they would lose money. Sounds brutal, right? No need to look for the major catch here. You **don't** get any money from the certificates they sell even though you are providing all the services! Bright Ideas Marketing keeps all the money, you just get the new patient.

I chose to look at it much differently. I figured that if ten people came into my office, I would definitely be able to diagnose, treatment plan, and educate them on their dental needs and that it would be worthwhile. Turns out that I was right! I saw over thirty-seven new patients that month, and I did make a profit even though I literally gave away free Zoom teeth whitening. In the following months, I received forty to sixty new patients a month, primarily from this marketing campaign. I can't say it enough: YOU NEED TO GET PEOPLE INTO YOUR OFFICE. At the time of this offer in 2005, this deal was excellent for Zoom whitening and still is.

Never underestimate the value of a new patient, a returning patient, or just a body in your office. Get them into your office!

So, how do you go about doing this? What is the most effective way to get people into your gorgeous, top-of-the-line office so that they can learn about your talent as a genuine super dentist, and experience your caring team? Not to mention, become aware the wide range of your dental services.

Here is the key element to marketing your services and getting people into your office. We agreed that marketing is consistently adding massive value to your patients, right? So, if you approach it from this mind-set, then at what most basic level can you begin to add this value? Begin by offering the services that patients *want*.

Market the services and products that people *want* and *desire*, not **what they** *need*.

Sorry to break it to your "dental mind" if you think people want root canals, crowns, bridges, fillings, exams, and x-rays. Now, I know what you are thinking. *How can he say that? He's a dentist! Isn't that what dentistry is all about? Providing the services that patients need?* The answer is *yes*. You're right! But consumer research shows that people love buying what they want and not what they think they need, just because it's good for them. Let's talk about some of the factors that determine your patients' wants.

Below I've listed some wants along with the mentality components that accompany those wants. To clarify, every want or desire has attached to it a certain mentality or psychological mind-set that fuels it. If you tap into your patients' wants based on a psychology that is fueling their wants, then your ability to market or add tremendous value to your patients increases dramatically.

Here are the areas that your marketing should focus on that expresses your patients' WANTS:

- **Great health:** An emotional component. Your health is the wealth that makes it possible for you to experience life to the highest standards.
- **Vitality:** An emotional component. Good dental health contributes to other healthy systems.
- **Beautiful smiles:** An emotional component. Patients look better and smile more often, which makes them feel better emotionally.
- **White smiles:** An emotional component. Patients feel better when their teeth are whiter.

- **Confidence when they smile:** An emotional component. Confidence breeds success in other areas of patients' lives.
- **Healthy mouths without bleeding gums:** A logical and emotional component. When one area is improved, so is another.
- **Fresh breath:** An emotional component. Bad breath makes patients uncomfortably self-conscious and limits socialization.
- **Straight teeth:** An emotional component. In our culture, straight teeth make patients feel better about their smile and self-image.

Do you get it? What do all of the above wants have in common? They are *all driven by emotion.* People want services and treatments that make them feel great about themselves and excite them. These are the types of items that people *BUY.* Don't you think it would be smart to base your marketing strategy on the top or common emotionally-based items and correlate them with the specific dental procedures to determine what they want? Don't get me wrong. I know that people may even want root canals and crowns and fillings, but there is a greater demand for those emotionally-based wants listed above.

No one needs a root canal; they *want* one because they are in pain. They want to be *pain-free* and in *good health* again. But these patients(root canal patients) are fewer than patients who *want* whitening, *want* that space closed with an implant, and *want* a better, straighter smile. Yes, they *want* a crown since their tooth cracked, but only because it is a dental emergency and to ignore it would compromise their dental health. You see, even this person who you may think wants a crown is really doing it because they feel the end result would give them a healthier mouth and overall better dental health. *People want to feel a certain way, help them feel that way.*

It's interesting to see just how much psychology influences our services and the mind-set involved when evaluating what patients really want from us. So, what services could dentists provide that would satisfy those psychological triggers that fuel a patient's wants? Here's a short list of sought-after treatments:

- Invisalign
- Teeth whitening
- Porcelain veneers

- Cosmetic reshaping of anterior teeth
- Gentle, easy, and regular teeth cleaning
- Continual dental information and education from a dentist
- Implant dentistry
- Information on teeth, health, well-being, lifestyle, and nutrition

You get them in for what they really *WANT* and then use your dental exam and knowledge to *EDUCATE* and *MOTIVATE* them on what they truly *NEED* according to your dental diagnosis.

Once you get patients into your office for what they *want* and not what you think they *need*, then the magic can happen. Why does this work so effectively? It's simple: you are focusing on their wants and educating and motivating them on their needs. When you educate them on what they truly need, then who are they going to trust to get that tooth restored when they are ready for treatment? You, of course. Notice that I said "motivating them on their needs." That's right. It's your responsibility to *motivate* your patients on treatments you think they really need. We will review the importance of motivation when we talk about treatment plan psychology in the next chapter.

Now, let's review some offers that give patients what they *want*. When creating offers and campaigns to bring patients into your office, focus on how you can present your services in unique ways while adding tremendous value to your patients.

The traditional advice is simply "Ask and you shall receive." I want you to remove this way of thinking from your psychology and replace it with something much more powerful, something that will leave a lasting effect in the minds of your patients.

Give generously and you shall receive in abundance.

Here are some offers and setups that harness the important elements that we have already reviewed:

Zoom whitening promo: This is a fail-proof, ultra-successful marketing piece since we are focusing on their wants, whiter teeth, and a healthier, more confident smile. So, if we advertised that $150 would get you teeth whitening treatment, that's a pretty darn good deal. But if we also added in that promotion exam, x-rays, and teeth whitening at only $150, this would be even better. This piece has worked flawlessly for me time and time again since it relies primarily on what my patient *wants*. Now, what if we added even more to all of this? Let's say we shot a quick three-minute video on how to keep your teeth whiter by avoiding certain foods and then, at the end of the video, we promoted a package deal that included the exam, x-rays, and teeth whitening for only $150? This would create even more value for your prospective patients since your goal is to add massive value to them. It's a very powerful way to get patients into your office for something they *want*. **Always remember, your patients' wants are tied to an emotional result.** In this case, it's a great-looking smile that gives them the confidence in their appearance.

I ran this same promotion through our local weekly magazine, such as the PennySaver, when I opened my first office in 2005. I would always get twenty to thirty-five new patients a month, roughly 200 to 300 patients a year. Obviously, back then, video marketing wasn't as common. I currently run online promotions that have triple the response rate. I know I mentioned the use of video and online marketing already, but we will really dive deep into this in a later section; it's a part of marketing that I really love. For right now, understand that you have to be adding value to their specific *want*-based services before your potential patients will come see you.

Chamber of Commerce: Going to your local Chamber of Commerce meeting every week is a great way to introduce yourself to the community. When you do go, make sure you take your office manager with you as well. I received at least ten to fifteen patients from the local chamber who have referred countless others over the years. When you do exchange information with names and e-mail, let them know that you will call them to set up an appointment. Don't assume they'll call you first. A great way to add some value to them before you make that call is to send them a short video with some useful content. An example would be the best toothbrush to use, or even something else related to dentistry that patients may ask you about. We will review this in great detail later in the book. Follow up with them, and have your office manager take the initiative by calling them to get them in. At first, you might feel a little uncomfortable sending people material, but it's quite simple. Once you have their e-mail, add their contact information to your automatic e-mailer, which will send them some really useful information about their dental health. We will walk through the setup later in the book.

Facebook ads: This is another targeted way to attract patients. You could use Trojan Insurance software to target local businesses on Facebook with specific deals for employees of that company. Facebook is great because it allows you to target the types of patients you want in your office. More on this later.

Social promotions: Today, social promotions are my preference when getting patients into my office. It is one of the best ways to add instant value to your prospective patients who may be viewing your promotion. Basically, hundreds of thousands of subscribers get an e-mail with a daily or short-term deal on a service your practice offers. Potential patients click on the deal in their e-mail and read how many other people have purchased that same deal and also how long the deal will be offered. The reach is limitless, and the out-of-pocket cost is nothing. Depending on which company you use, you don't pay anything until someone buys the deal. Currently, there are so many online social deal makers out there. Here are just a few of them:

- Groupon
- Living Social
- PennySaver's SaverTime
- Screamin' Daily Deals
- Dealgrind

These social promotions are a great way to boost a large volume of new patients. Before you do though, there are certain key elements of your online presence you should be aware of because, as fast as they spread the word about your location, they can also create bad press if you are not set up correctly to accept their response. We will go into the details of setting up your online presence prior to using these marketing platforms. For right now, know that they are very powerful tools in marketing your services, and for maximum influence in your practice you need to first consider other areas of impact in the *business of your practice*.

Market to local businesses using Trojan Insurance software: With Trojan Insurance software, you can search most insurance plans under local business names and look up their insurance coverage. For example, if you look up Starbucks and notice they have a great PPO plan, you can then design a one-page insurance sheet and give it to all the local Starbucks employees as a special promotion from the local dental practice (you!).

Dry cleaners are also great because they draw a lot of foot traffic. Go to your local dry cleaners and ask if you can place a promotional box on their countertop in exchange for something. As people are waiting to pick up their clothes, they can enter a contest by placing their name and e-mail address in the box. Every week, pick up the box and e-mail them some value-added content, and then follow up with a phone call to schedule them for an appointment. This strategy worked very well at one of our local dry cleaners, thanks to my office manager who followed up with all those inquiries. Don't do this with just one business in your community; do it with several.

This strategy can be very powerful if you contact large businesses through their human resources department and emphasize that your office takes their dental plan. Express to them that you are willing to come down and do a quick overview of their dental insurance and answer any questions they may have about their teeth. You can do this in a couple of hours in the afternoon and hand out disposable whitening trays to those who are there. You can also express to them that by focusing on preventative dentistry, their employees will be more likely to miss fewer days at work and be more pain-free as well. Some companies will even allow you to place your cards and information in their staff lounges.

Communities and schools: Get to know your local community clubs and organizations, such as city hall, churches, retirement homes, golf clubs, tennis clubs, swimming teams, and so on. You can sponsor events and give out complimentary exams, x-rays, and deals on in-office teeth whitening. This is a smart way to attract local patients.

So, after you've gotten them into your office, what's next? Are you done *attracting* them yet? Is it time to move on to our treatment plan stage? Absolutely not. The treatment plan stage starts when you perform their dental exam and not a minute before. Once they're in your office, keep in mind it's just a foot in the door and means nothing unless they actually *like* what they see. Your front office staff must connect with them, endorse you as their dentist, and express interest in their lives and well-being.

How can we do this in the short time we have with them? To start, train your front office staff how to implement the techniques listed below. Emphasize to them that no matter how many times a patient comes to your office, these techniques, if implemented properly, will continue to ATTRACT your patients for years to come.

5 TRAINABLE TECHNIQUES TO CONNECT WITH ANY PATIENT THAT COMES TO YOUR OFFICE

1. **Give them world-class service** from the moment they call your office and walk through your doors. Take care of them: ask if they'd like some water, a magazine, a blanket, a toothbrush, or for the staff to arrange a ride back for them.

2. **Bring up a mutual interest and document.** This is HUGE! It's so easy to connect with someone when you have a mutual interest. Ask questions to learn about what your patients do on their weekends or what they've got planned after they leave the office. Write this down in the chart so that you can connect with them during future appointments. They will appreciate that you cared and remembered.

3. **Give a gift, give a referral, pay a compliment, or make a startling statement.** Some gifts that we give out in my offices are Starbucks cards, take-home teeth whitening trays, or even dinner certificates to local restaurants. Give a sample of something. Give them an important phone number, a referral to something you both like, such as a restaurant or even a new dental product that your office just got in. One of my patients always talks to me about his scuba diving lessons and trips. He knows that I would love to scuba dive one day so now *he* is sending me info on it. This type of rapport goes beyond just small talk; it really *connects*. When I say *startling statement*, I mean something different

that will catch their attention, something positive that creates good conversation.

4. **Tell a story.** People love stories that might reveal who you really are. Make sure it is something short, positive, and entertaining.

5. **Ask questions, listen, and document!** Remember, people love to talk about themselves, so *let them!* Instruct your team to ask your patients fun and nonintimidating questions about their days or some activities they've done recently. When you gradually and comfortably ask them about their lives, always *document this in their charts and read it before you see them again.* This way, you can bring up some of those points during casual conversation.

These are small ways that your team can instantly connect with your patients; these are also some of the biggest reasons that I don't like having flat-screen TVs in the reception area. When patients walk in, they become glued to the TV, which discourages your team from interacting with them. We are already inundated with so many distractions; instead of distracting patients in your reception area, interact with them and make a personal connection. If you want to put educational material up on a flat screen, use an iPad in the back office while they wait for you. Just make sure you play relevant videos about useful tips and tricks to help them have better health and teeth. We'll talk more about this later.

All of this will be done within the confines of your state-of-the-art office. Make sure you review the *Psychology of a World-Class Office Design* section to make the necessary modifications to your practice. Even if you are not building a practice from scratch, you can still use elements from that section and modify what you've got. Also, make sure you understand all of the design principles and successful team building aspects as it all affects your ability to attract patients.

The take-home message is that patient attraction leaves a lasting impression once they actually come into your office and create healthy relationships with your team. There is a *psychology* that *gradually builds* to set you up for very successful treatment plans.

Chapter 11

TREATMENT PLAN
PSYCHOLOGY

Treat them with your plan; don't plan them with your treatment.

Your patients seek you out and reach out to you. They go to your website and make an appointment, or they pick up the phone and call your office to schedule an appointment. They've already looked at their schedules and made sure they can get time off work; they've appointed a babysitter to watch the kids; they've scheduled a few hours away from their spouse; and they've rescheduled meetings—all of this so that they can walk around numb for hours afterward. Then, they drive to your office, locate your suite, and fill out a bunch of paperwork (if they haven't already done it online). Then, they sit in your chair so that you can evaluate their dental health. Phew! They've done a lot just to be there with you. This doesn't even include the psychological component of the stress of a dental appointment. What they *don't* want is to find another dentist and repeat the same laborious cycle again. Don't give them a reason to seek treatment elsewhere. Trust me, they don't want go home without some sort of treatment, whether it be a whitening, cleaning, restorative, or even crown and bridge. They came there for you to evaluate their oral condition and contribute to their health in some way.

THE PSYCHOLOGY OF TREATMENT PRESENTATION

In the previous chapter, we emphasized attracting patients to your office based on what they *want* and then *educating and motivating* them on what they need. So, what is *motivation* anyway?

In dental school, you were never taught the importance of motivation in influencing your patients to make better decisions about their dental health. So, what is motivation when it comes to treatment?

Motivation is having patients energized and internally aligned with your reasons for suggesting the treatment you diagnosed.

To do this, you must first align with them or, in other words, gain *clear congruency* with them and then lead them to the place you want. For example, if you are talking to the patient on the phone or in person, and they have a very subtle tone and demeanor, you should create a rapport with them by mirroring their tone and demeanor. Once you are aligned with them, you can influence them much more effectively. Find out what makes them respond. Be present, watch them, listen to them, and lead them to a healthy place. You can't align with someone else until you have mastered your own emotions; your treatment plan presentation depends on this.

Before you can perfect your treatment plan presentation, you must first master the art of *harnessing your emotional capacity* to make sure you are in the best state of mind. Having a patient in your office and having them in the dental chair open to your suggestions are two different things. It's one thing to get them in the office, but it's an entirely different psychology to have them see the *value* in taking action. When a patient sits down in your chair, have the mind-set to connect with them on *their level,* or else you will lose the ability to build and earn their trust through the process.

In dentistry, the number one reason patients will do treatment with you is that they feel they TRUST you, and BELIEVE you are looking out for their best interest. Not your pocketbook's.

The importance of being in the best physiological and mental state of mind prior to entering a room where your patient is waiting is often understated. I know you may think this is an overkill if you have been practicing dentistry for thirty years, but this perspective still applies. Your patient doesn't deserve (nor do they want) thirty years of your emotional output; *they deserve 100 percent of your attention and presence at this very moment.*

You need to bring some enthusiasm and energy into that treatment room from the very beginning of your contact with that patient. To be successful at treatment planning your patients effectively, you must always be moving to that place of excellence and success in your own life. Too many doctors bring their lives into the treatment room, and it casts a negative shadow on the patient, which is unacceptable. When you walk into the room, bring your greatness in with you! I say this from a totally humble perspective and refer to the term *greatness* to indicate your inner success. So many patients have commented on how happy I am when I first meet them. They say that it was my happiness and positive attitude that got them to commit to doing treatment with me; they want to be around that, and *they trust the source that brings that happiness into the room.*

Too many dentists walk into the room thinking that all their cool technology, dental knowledge, and CE courses will make their patients love them. This couldn't be farther from the truth. Skills, tactics, and specialized knowledge don't make you great; it's something else.

Darren Hardy, publisher of *SUCCESS* magazine, features and interviews the world's most extraordinary achievers. Below I've listed what he indentifies as some of the most common personal characteristics that these high achievers have. He categorizes these qualities in one of three ways to improving yourself: skills and tactics, specialized knowledge, and attitude. Any quality you can think of can be identified as an area of improvement in your skills and tactics, specialized knowledge, or attitude. Here are some of the qualities that *SUCCESS* magazine found that the most extraordinary achievers posses:

QUALITIES	AREAS OF IMPROVEMENT
Passionate	Attitude
Persistent	Attitude
Integrity	Attitude
Vision	Attitude
Purpose	Skill and Attitude
Giver	Attitude
Risk-taker	Attitude
Contribution	Attitude
Habits	Skill
Energy	Attitude
Focus	Skill and Attitude
Discipline	Skill

Note that out of the twelve qualities above, eight of them are purely attitude-based, and the other four are *a skill* or a mix of both *skill and attitude.* Also note that *specialized knowledge* doesn't apply to any of the above. Don't get me wrong here; we can't be ignorant of the fact that you need to know how to prep the distobuccal of #15, and it's assumed that you do. But the attribute that contributes to your success is your attitude, or, better said, your *championship mind-set.* So, learn and understand the psychology of the treatment plan presentation before we jump into the details of your treatment plan.

SELLING VS. BUYING

Goods and products are exchanged in two ways. The first is when someone *sells* the product to you. The second is when someone *buys* the product from you. In every case, anyone wanting to exchange a product or service of any sort would rather have the patient there to *buy from them* rather than having to *sell* the product to that patient. Always keep that rule in mind when discussing a treatment plan.

When a patient decides to buy from you, it means that you or someone in their world has set off certain psychological triggers that have convinced them that your product or service is more valuable to them than the money they are paying you for it.

My point is that your patients should *buy from you* instead of you *selling to them*. When someone is *buying* from you, they *want* what you are providing. When you are *selling* to someone, you are *pushing* your ideology or perspective on them in order for them to see it your way. Here are some examples in our society of what people want to *buy*:

First, let's start with some retail examples:

Purses: Coach, Louis Vuitton
Sunglasses: Gucci, Prada, Chanel
Cars: Mercedes-Benz, BMW, Ferrari, Porsche, Lamborghini
Technology: iPad, iPhone, Mac computers

Remember the examples of services you can provide in your office that people want?:

Invisalign
Teeth whitening
Porcelain veneers
Cosmetic reshaping of anterior teeth
Gentle, easy, and regular teeth cleaning
Continual dental information and education from a dentist
Implant dentistry
Information on their teeth, health, wellbeing, lifestyle, and nutrition.
Emergency dentistry
Dental sleep medicine

These are some of the most common dental services you can provide your patients. These are all *buyer services*, services that patients request. These services usually don't require you to push your patients into considering them. Yes, there may be a financial agreement you will have to come to, but for the most part no selling is involved here. People come in wanting these services because something in their world has convinced them that what they are buying will make them feel a certain way and resolve something internal. *Never sell to your patients; always have them want and buy your services.*

How do you do this? First, you must understand *WHY PEOPLE BUY*.

What triggers the buying of a service or product? Buying a service or product has always and will always have an emotional component that accompanies it. Patients know that taking care of their oral health makes them feel a certain way, and getting specific treatments done may represent something to them. Having a better smile and a sense of health gives them a sense of certainty, significance, and even connection with themselves and others. There is an overwhelming emotional component when it comes to making buying decisions. ***Therefore, integrate the emotional <u>result</u> of your services into your treatment plan.***

Below are just a few emotional results of great dentistry while establishing a deep connection with your patients:

Straight teeth: It's also a sense of emotional awareness, the *knowingness* that patients' teeth are straight does a lot for their self-image.

White, beautiful smiles: A sense a beauty is conveyed by whiter teeth.

Confidence: Patients express themselves with their smile. Greater confidence is due to other people noticing their teeth, making them feel good because they know *others* think their teeth and smile look attractive.

Healthy mouths: Patients won't have bleeding gums and will not be embarrassed by bad breath.

Great health: This is an emotional sense of being that every patient wants to achieve. Patients' overall health is better as a result of consistent oral health care.

Vitality: Vitality comes when patients can smile with confidence because of reassurance from others. A sense of vitality can also come from confidently being able to eat the right foods since you have healthy enough teeth to chew your foods effectively. Let's not forget that poor occlusion can lead to digestive problems from food that is not properly chewed!

Fresh breath: This eliminates self-doubt in social situations and boosts confidence with significant others.

Certainty: This is an emotion that emergency dentistry can bring about. Certainty is comfort in knowing that pain will cease once treatment is complete.

Laughter: Patients will laugh more because their teeth look and feel great. Giving your patients the gift and freedom to smile and laugh with family and friends heightens satisfaction in their lives.

For instance, if they are contemplating getting that crown redone because it has a black line at the gingiva, encourage them by telling them they will feel more naturally confident when smiling knowing that no one is focusing on that black metal line. Talk to them about how bacteria adhere to rough metal surfaces more than they do to a polished, smooth porcelain surface. Also, tell them that by keeping a defective crown in their mouth, they are slowly destroying their smile line. Do you see how there are two emotional phrases built into our treatment plan here? The first is the natural, confident smile and the other is the more clinically associated bacteria, which destroys their smile line. So, what's the answer here? What's the solution to their problem? Getting a new functionally aesthetic porcelain crown and feeling *confident* and *certain* about their smile. People come to buy Confidence and Certainty, not porcelain crowns. That's the buyer's truth.

> *Don't focus on the seller's hustle; instead, focus on the buyer's truth by attaching the emotional result to your service.*

Okay, this all sounds great, but what exactly is *buying?*

BUYING IS EMOTION IN *MOTION*

Buying is the *transference of emotion.* It's the transference of emotion from the dentist who has the goods and services to the one who *might* want them: the patient. *Buying is emotion in motion.* Patients will choose you because they trust you, like you, have confidence in you, and think you can successfully treat them. Most important, they believe you have their best interest at heart. As you can see, there are a lot of emotional qualities wrapped up in the above statement: trust, connection, friendliness, certainty, and security. Did you ever think a dental procedure would have such prerequisites? Trust, connection, friendliness, certainty, and security are the five prerequisites, or emotions, you must convey to your patients when you enter that room to do an exam, a treatment plan, or a procedure. Simply put, patients buy from dentists they trust and feel connected to.

THE 5 EMOTIONAL QUALITIES YOU MUST ALWAYS CONVEY TO YOUR PATIENTS DURING AN EXAM, TREATMENT PLAN, OR PROCEDURE

1. **Trust:** It all starts here. Be honest. Tell your patients if you don't know something but, at the same time, tell them you will find out. Tell them the negatives of getting some treatments done as well. So, do tell them that in a veneer, you can trim off 0.5–1.0 mm of tooth structure. Be up front with your treatment agenda and outcomes. But, when you do, also convey to your patients a sense of certainty.

2. **Certainty:** Your patients need certainty that you can do what you are suggesting. How do you speak during your treatment plan? Are there lots of *ums, oohs,* and *huhs*? How is your posture? If someone was listening to your voice from another room, would you *sound* as certain as you think you are? You must answer *yes* to these questions to convey *certainty* to your patients. Please don't mistake *certainty* for *arrogance*. Stay humble, but be certain. Remember that certainty is also admitting that you are unsure of something but that you will find the answer. In dental medicine or in any branch of health care, you will not always *know* everything. So, part of your certainty is *acknowledging and being wise in your unknowing.*

3. Friendliness: This is an emotional quality of universal desire. Everyone loves friendliness. Be friendly, know that you're their dentist, but also look at them like you are their friend. People like having good friends. Be professional and don't cross any professional boundaries, but interact with them as a good friend would. By doing this, you are forming a connection with them.

4. Connection/Presence: When patients trust you and sense that you are a friendly person, they will also feel a connection with you. Build rapport with your patients. *To do this, you must first fit into their world.* If your patient is soft-spoken, realize it and don't come into the room with a loud, overbearing voice. Instead, use a lighter, but firm and friendly voice that better fits into their world. Instead of shocking them with your presence, gradually take them where you want them to go emotionally. Being in their world with them will make them feel safe and secure. Being focused on them and being fully present while you are in the room will give you a deeper and meaningful connection with your patients. Remember to give them 100% of your attention, not just fragments of it.

5. Security: You and your office environment should convey a sense of safety and security. We talked about the psychology of a world-class office and the importance of designing a suite that is non-intimidating. This also means making it safe. What do the chairs look like? Where are the instruments, and can your patients see them? Do you have blankets or provide safety glasses while you do treatment? Do you listen to them when you come into the room, or is *your* agenda the agenda they must follow? Is your operatory clean? Did you seat them in a closed room, or is it open yet private? Do they see the same dentist every time they come to your office, which helps to eliminate surprise and uncertainty? Do you verbally express to your patients that you and your staff will do everything possible to accommodate them? Some of these actions may be very subtle, but don't undermine the importance and message that they can deliver by creating that feeling of safeness and wellbeing when they are within the reach of your care. Every *patient* wants this.

COMMUNICATION

Realize that all of these emotions are dependent upon how you communicate with your patients. Understanding styles of communication, both verbal and non-verbal, is integral to your success when you meet a new patient or treat a regular one.

Research has proven that communication is split into three main modalities: verbal, tonality, and physiological. Which one do you think contributes most to what's communicated? You'll be surprise to learn that the verbal portion is in the minority when it comes to communicating. Your physiology, or physical form, accounts for about 56% of what you communicate to your patients. This would include how you move your body, your hands, and even your smile. 33% comes from your tone, and 11% is verbal. If you think about it, this is counterintuitive—a shocking truth about communication.

Most of us go to school and learn about verbal communication, which is what we actually *say*. And dental school focuses on content-driven curricula. But if you went into the room with your patients and addressed them in a monotone, non-physiologically stimulating, yet prolific and content-driven voice, then patients would write you off as a dentist who lacked all social skills. Your power to have them see value in what you do would diminish greatly. Henceforth, they would be less likely to buy dental services from you. Don't agree? Think about the most successful people you know in any field. When you talk to them about their topic or expertise, don't they light up and display a sense of presence and focus that conveys their authority? Isn't it their *tone* that communicates a point? Aren't they deliberate in their *movements* when they talk? You should harness these same skills and continually build this art form when communicating anything to your patients. They see you as the *EXPERT*. Now communicate to them in that way!

BEST STATE = BEST PHYSIOLOGY

When it comes to physiology, remember this tip:

The most effective way to transfer that emotion to your patient is by controlling your physiological and mental state.

Remember, people associate your state to your service, brand, or product, which means if you're in a negative physiological and mental state, your patients will associate those negative feelings to your treatment or office. In addition, your own state of mind affects your treatment suggestions for a particular patient. In other words, the way you are (your tone and demeanor) is what you're prescribing to your patient. If you are passionate and *present* while talking to your patients, they pick up on that and link it to their treatment. Look at it from this perspective: how your patients feel when they leave your office is also the product or treatment that you are selling. Be excited about seeing them and explaining ways to do healthy treatments. If you are talking about a restorative procedure, show some passion for it, or explain with enthusiasm how RCT instrumentation is much different today than what they have heard or experienced in the past. Be *ecstatic* that you have the opportunity to help them improve their smile, look, and oral health!

I know that we've covered a lot in this chapter. Let's keep the key points in mind as we move forward. We started by saying that you must have the right mind-set, perspective, and attitude to succeed with your patients; these are necessary components to breed success. In addition, we've gained a deeper understanding of treatment plan psychology by identifying what buying treatment is all about and why we should link emotional results to treatment acceptance. Finally, we learned the five key emotions we must convey to patients as well as the three basic ways we communicate to our patients, all of which we use to refine our treatment planning psychology.

Now, let's learn about specific treatment planning practices that positively impact case acceptance, patient satisfaction, and confidence in our diagnoses.

Chapter 12

TREATMENT PLAN INSIGHTS

God is in the details.

TREATMENT PLAN

Now that you've learned about the emotional and psychological triggers in yourself and your patients, you are ready to explore the *winning mechanics* behind a successful treatment plan, which will solidify your bond with your patient. Let's move on to the second stage in the ATR System: Treatment Planning.

So where does this put you? It puts you in a place of influence. You must have an educational influence on your patients when reviewing their treatment plan. When you meet them you strive to have a happy, vibrant, and forward-thinking influence on them. You want them to know that you don't care how long it's been since they've seen the dentist. All that matters is that they are here now, and they are starting somewhere. When you greet them, make sure you look presentable, with no food or plaque on your teeth, and *make sure your mask is not over your mouth.*

I remember once I went in for a job interview with what seemed to be a very successful dentist with a nice office in a busy part of town. During the entire interview, he wore his face mask—for over twenty minutes. The interview was over, and I never saw his entire face. It was so impersonal. Make sure you don't come off like this with your patients. Greet them appropriately with their first name and a hand-shake, look them in the eye, and introduce yourself as Dr. SuperDentist. The first thing you should do is ask them something general like, "How are you today?" Then, say something interesting about who they remind you of or even something interesting about yourself. Get to know them for the first minute. *Discuss anything but dentistry.* This will lighten up the mood and put your patient at ease. Ask questions and *listen* to their answers. Then, give them an overview of what you will be doing next. Try something like this: "Well, this is gonna be a really easy appointment for you. We're gonna go over your x-rays, and then I'll take a look in your mouth and *sit you back up* so that we can discuss any concerns you might have." This gives them an idea about what to expect. It's also your subtle way of telling your patients that you're asking permission to exam their mouth. Notice that I said *"sit you back up."* I stress this because many dentists, still wearing their masks and loops, will discuss an entire treatment plan with patients while the patients are still reclined. How impersonal is that? Sit your patient upright, and resume your conversation. Let's break it down:

1. Greet your patients.
2. Discuss anything but dentistry.
3. Ask questions about *them*.
4. Provide them with an overview of today's appointment.

When you first look into their mouth, either say something positive or say nothing at all. Some dentists say something like, "Oh, looks like you haven't gotten your teeth cleaned in a while." Or, "Has it been some time since your last cleaning?" The second remark is not as direct, but geez, how is that going to make your patient feel? Not too comfortable, I'd imagine. Try this instead: "Okay, let's take a look here," or "Alright, looking good," or "Nice teeth," or even "You've got some good dental work, but let me point out a concern here." Always give your patients a mirror to point anything out. As you make notes in their chart, tell them you'll review your notes with them after you are done. Sit them up, *and then* review the entire treatment plan with them. It's not likely that patients on their back will be inclined to make any major buying decisions regarding their teeth; in this position, they are at a disadvantage. So, sit them up and work with them. Connect with them here, and *then* lead the way. Be cognizant of the five emotions that you must convey to every patient.

I want to review one main point that you should keep in mind while mastering the art of these twenty-one treatment plan insights. Here it is: *always be consistent in your practice.* That is, create a consistent experience for your patients every time they come to your office.

Michael Gerber, the author of *E-Myth Revisited*, talks about the importance of consistency with your customers. Consistency in your dental practice is no different. So many variables affect patients that consistency must be a priority in your practice. People want consistency; it indicates value when they see you perform the same procedures every time they come in. Let's say, for example, you are about to start treatment and your protocol is to have patients wear protective eyewear every time. In order to create that value here make sure you or one of your assistants gives them protective eyewear before their treatment begins. Don't do it sometimes or seven out of ten times. Do it all the time. If your front office team offers water to the patient upon arriving, make sure they do it all the time. If you verbally assure them immediately before winding up the handpiece and use certain phrases, make sure you tell them *every* time, exactly at that specific time using your usual tone and manner. Consistency of experience for a patient indicates a standard or a value that your practice is linked to. Not only is it a gauge to evaluate value with every experience, it's a performance indicator as well. Keep consistency of experience in mind as you review the twenty-one treatment plan insights below.

21 TREATMENT PLAN INSIGHTS TO TRIPLE YOUR CASE ACCEPTANCE

I call these *insights* since it took me many years to learn from these light bulb moments. When I made the connection and actually put them to use, the results were astonishing. Three times the number of patients accepted treatment when I utilized these treatment plan tricks. Sometimes making the smallest difference in how you present something has the biggest impact on the result.

This is a *presentation*, not a let-me-go-over-fees-with-you session so you can do treatment with us! If your patients aren't accepting treatment, first ask yourself what you could have done better. Remember, you are not a salesperson; your goal is for them to buy treatment from you, not to sell it to them. If you effectively use these treatment plan tips and tricks, you will have more influence on your patients, and you will leave them feeling richer and more educated about their oral health. In return, patients will seek out your suggestions for treatment. Here are some amazing tips and tricks while creating treatment plans for your patients. Some of these are simple, and others are a bit more involved; but if you use just a few of them in your practice, your treatment plan acceptance will soar!

TIP #1: Speak their language. You must always remember when doing treatment plans that patients like to know exactly what you're talking about in *their* language, not yours. You can teach them the dental terminology, but first get them acquainted with what is happening using terms that they can relate to. For example, don't use the phrase *class V abrasions*; instead, use *areas of wear* or *wedges on your teeth near your gum line*. Too many dentists graduate dental school and forget that patients don't speak *dental*. You'll lose them if you don't speak their language. This also includes being very careful identifying teeth with their associated numbers, instead point to areas in their mouth then follow that up with a tooth number.

TIP #2: The Class V Mock Up. When you are diagnosing class V abrasions and telling patients what they are and what one will look like, always use the flowable composite (no bonding agent), a curing light, and place one on their tooth and show them what it would look like after it is done. Place it on so it's not too rough since you don't really have to polish it; just place it and cure it. Then, give them a mirror so that they can see what you just did. Now, they actually have a visual of what it will look like when you are done. The same could apply to showing them a quick chair-side mock-up of what their veneers could look like when they elected to do them.

TIP #3: Use a mirror. When most patients go to the dentist, they are *told* what they need but are never *shown* what they need. Intra-oral cameras are great and you should use them but only in conjunction with a hand mirror. After you are done examining their teeth, while they are still lying flat, give them a mirror and show them your concerns. The mirror gives them a reference point that is magnified. Then, if you follow up with an intra-oral after you sit them up and relate that to what you showed them in the mirror, it's a double whammy! When patients look at intra-oral images of their teeth, they may not always have a perfect directional orientation of their mouth, but if you told them that you pointed that out in the mirror and that's what they are looking at in the intra-oral images on the screen, they now have a point of reference. Remember, patients don't look at teeth all day long like you do.

TIP #4: Always walk them out. You should take the time to walk your patients out to the reception area after treatment and explain what they can expect at their next appointment. This is a nice personal touch, and it shows that you care.

TIP #5: Use their name. When you first meet your patient, walk into the room and say, "Hi, Chris. How are you doing today? I'm Dr. SuperDentist." Most dentists just walk into the room and introduce themselves without even using the patient's name. Even worse, they walk in and do neither. You need to create an impression during those first two minutes. Communicate that you are energetic, happy, and excited to see them because they are all that you are focusing on. Be present. Be there with them, not just in front of them.

TIP #6: Go over Proxy Brush uses. Most patients are never told the most obvious and simple things they can do to improve their oral health. Dentists are graduating in the most technologically advanced age ever. Still, your patients don't want you to overlook the small stuff. Proxy brushes and floss threaders(if needed) are often overlooked when it comes to instructing our patients on oral hygiene. Sounds really trivial and small, but this can be a distinction that really leaves your patients feeling like you actually do care about their teeth when they leave your office.

TIP #7: Show them the technology. If you have some cool technology or gadgets in your office, show it to your patients. Don't just tell them about it.

TIP #8: Sit your patients upright for treatment plan presentations. Sit them upright in their chairs, and then review the treatment plan with them. I know we have mentioned this before but I included it here again since it's so often overlooked, yet so important. There are so many dentists out there who are used to talking to their patients while they are still lying flat in the chair. Think about it, that is a very submissive and weak position to be in and how likely is it that they will be making major financial buying decisions about their teeth from a weak point. Sit em up make them feel like they have some control over things and be on their level. Connect with them here, *then* take them to where you want them to go.

TIP #9: Have an immaculate operatory. This one is pretty obvious! Patients will buy more frequently and with greater comfort if they know that your practice and treatment rooms are clean. Before you bring patients back, make sure you don't have any gauze, cotton pellets, or cement on the floor. Make sure the cords to all your equipment are clean, and get an evaluation of what that operatory looks like by sitting in that chair and looking all around you to see if you can notice anything that was missed. Be detailed here; clean up the corners of the room, the all too often spit-spotted overhead light, and replace any water-damaged ceiling tiles. We are often complimented on how clean our office is kept. Patients want your office to be clean and sterile, and they feel more comfortable when they know you are keeping it that way.

TIP #10: Insert instead of inlay. When you are talking to your patients about porcelain inlays and onlays, use *porcelain insert* instead of *inlay* or *onlay*. Most people aren't familiar with this type of terminology. When you use visually descriptive words, your patients will understand what you are talking about. Apply this technique for any treatment procedure to make it easy for your patients to understand and remember the names of specific dental treatments.

TIP #11: Always ask where they heard about you. This one is really important. Don't forget to ask how they found you. Was it through their insurance, Facebook, YouTube, a friend, their church, Twitter, Yelp, or some other online avenue? Once you know how the word is getting out about you and your practice, you will feel more confident about marketing to those places.

Tip #12: Apologize. This is meant specifically for patients who tell you they had a horrible experience at some other dentist's office. This is your chance to take some responsibility for your industry by saying, "I'm sorry you had such a negative experience. I promise that we'll make it totally different for you here. Feel free to let me know if there is anything I or my team can do to make you feel more comfortable." When you apologize for someone else in your field, you rise above the whole industry. You are telling your patients that you set your own standard as high possible and are committed to delivering only the best.

TIP #13: Basics on x-rays. Always review with your patients the basic structures of their x-rays. Never display your patient's x-rays without showing them where the bone level is, identifying the enamel on their teeth, and an overall outlook on what you see on the x-rays. Most people have heard of enamel, point it out for them since it will give them some familiarity with what you are talking about. Make sure that the first thing you point out on their x-ray is not something negative, most times you can find something positive to say and then move forward from there.

TIP #14: Review OTC Dentistry. When you review what patients normally see over the counter, you become an expert in their eyes. You need to add expert input on normal everyday things. Some examples of this can be reviewing specific toothbrushes, rinses, or even new products that may be coming out on the market.

TIP #15: Give warranties. One of the most effective ways to convince someone to give you money or buy from you is to remove all the risk. Dentists are under the impression that they don't sell items that can be warranted, but don't you stand behind all the good work you do? If yes, then why not make it known and put your promise into your treatment plan package? Yes, package it up *into* your treatment plan. When your treatment coordinator is presenting treatments, have him or her go over the promise of service or warranties on all items presented. I give ten-year warranties on all Lava DVS crowns. My local lab, Okon laboratories, has a written declaration from 3M (makers of Lava) that if their crown cracks in half, chips, or shears, they will replace it at no cost for up to fifteen years. What a great idea! Why not expose this to our patients and package up a service plan or warranty on those types of items? So, we increased the price of our Lava crowns and included a warranty for up to ten years, taking the risk out of purchasing. People loved it. Yet, *most dentists still don't do it.*

Tip #16: Educate. This is a useful tip on so many levels. Remember, marketing means consistently adding massive value. In your treatment plan, you do this by educating your patients on what treatment they clinically need, and tie an emotional result to that as well. Earlier we talked about how you should get them into the office because of what they *want*, for services we called *buyer items*, but when you examine their teeth, you'll probably notice other services they need. In these situations, you must first educate them on why they need the treatment you're planning, and then attach the emotional result to actually getting it done. Let's say a patient wants to whiten his teeth and, after doing a full exam, you find that he needs a crown on tooth #8 since there is an open margin on the lingual. He came in because of the whitening, but now you have to educate him on what he *needs* by showing him that an open margin can damage the tooth underneath through recurrent decay.

Moreover, it can lead to a root canal and even tooth loss if left untreated. You then express that the best time to take care of it is before you whiten his teeth so that you can order the new crown from the lab to match it up with the newly whitened teeth. Do you see how this is coupling the educational *why* to the emotional result? *You bring them in for something they want and educate them on something they need, while connecting that to an emotional result.*

Tip #17: **Present treatment visually.** This is overlooked by dentists everywhere. We get so used to presenting the same treatment all the time to our patients, and because *we* know what we are doing and how it looks, we forget that patients don't fully understand what we are talking about. Use a model for porcelain inlays; use a periodontal model to show gum disease, bone grafts, scaling, and root planning; and you can even show your patients what a crowned tooth looks like. You assume your patients know exactly what you're talking about, but only when they see it can they place value on it and, as a result, are more comfortable paying you for it. This is not the same as using an intra-oral camera. Models show you the result of your treatment and the steps in between, and they are extremely effective. So, use them frequently, and keep them with you every time you do a treatment plan. Your patients will appreciate it and will comment that no one has ever taken the time to show them what their treatment looks like. I suggest you also have your treatment coordinator use them during treatment planning as well.

TIP #18: **Create mutual and healthy urgency.** Give patients a reason why they should pay today. Use a 5% pre-pay courtesy price reduction, or offer a complimentary product for them or a family member. What will happen if they don't take care of their teeth today? What happens if this promotion ends? Will it cost them more money? Maybe starting today will get their teeth looking their best before a big event such as a wedding. Maybe we can get them on the schedule a lot easier and quicker if they pay in full. We could also bill out their insurance before it is expires. Use these reasons as *leverage*! Don't be afraid of having a call-to-action to pay, in other words let them know what you want them to do today.

Tip #19: **Use third-party financing.** This is a no-brainer. Why wouldn't you present *every patient* with available financing options via CareCredit,

Chase Bank, or some of the other institutions out there? If you are going over treatment that costs $3,700, don't tell your patients their dental treatment will be $3,700; instead, say it will be around $300 per month for twelve months without interest. Present the best scenario. Don't hide the total cost, but don't be quick to throw out large numbers either. You don't want to make an alarming financial first impression, so keep it lighter first and then get deeper if they want to know the total cost. Tell them they can get approved through your office and, if they decide to do treatment, they won't get their first bill in the mail for a few weeks. This relieves people. It's not such a big commitment if they don't have to come up with any money that day. My offices prefer CareCredit, and I suggest you get used to working with such a company. Collecting money for treatment in full is worth the 10 percent finance fee they charge the practice.

TIP #20: Gain momentum. What happens next? Most dentists would say, "You gotta start their treatment." This is true, but how—and when? The best way to look at the next step is to focus on the psychology of *momentum*. You need to get *their* momentum going in order to get treatment done. Start today! Help them get a mental start on treatment. Don't have them come back next time. Suggest to them that they can start today with something small, anything that will get the process started; this builds momentum, and now the next appointment will be that much easier to schedule. Anytime someone takes a small step toward a goal, attaining that end result becomes that much easier. If patients leave your office without doing anything, they still haven't mentally started their treatment. Your job is to help them take that baby step and get something started for them *today* while they are still in the chair.

TIP #21: Home with a plan. This is where you can really separate yourself from the rest of the pack. If your patient doesn't get treatment done that day and doesn't commit to anything, then what happens next? The first thing to ask yourself is where you could have improved your presentation and delivery. Second, make sure you have a documented plan to have the patient return. (We will discuss this at length in the next chapter.) Third, send them home with a treatment plan for the services they need, including a way to pay for them in one folder. If you use a third-party financier, such as CareCredit or Chase Bank, include that in their folder explaining the monthly payments necessary to get treatment done. Many patients have come back and told us we were the only office that actually printed out a treatment plan and a financial plan showing them a way to pay for the treatment, even though they had decided not to do treatment that day. Keep in mind that even if they don't start that day, they will keep that information with them. Doing this for your patients shows them you not only care about them today, but are willing to see them in the future as they consider the various treatment and financial options available to them. Send them home with a plan!

Your goal is to have your patients asking questions like this: "Okay, doc, what can I do to improve my situation? Can you suggest anything?" When your patients ask for your input and guidance, you've hit the mark. You've sparked their interest through treatments you've laid out for them.

The tips above will help you get your patient to that place. Remember what we said: patients come into your office because of something they want. *Then, it's your responsibility to educate them on what they may need while utilizing the motivation of an emotional result from that treatment. If educating them results in their seeing value in what you suggest, they will want to buy the treatment you have planned.*

Using the insights from above will increase your treatment plan acceptance dramatically. Now that you have more patients in treatment, you have to follow up with the ones you've treated and also create a plan of return for the ones that you haven't. Let's pave their path back to the office!

Chapter 13

RETURN AND REFER

*Those who know and trust you will buy from you time and time again,
if only we focused on them and not on the strangers.*

Most dentists place their focus on attracting new patients. But the majority of your time and effort should be spent adding value to your existing patients. Market to them, contribute to them, and have them return and refer.

The ATR System is a powerful way to fuel your practice with the strategies you need for growth. Now that you know how to attract and treatment plan your patients, what happens when they've received treatment and have gone home, or, worse, they haven't received treatment at all? This is one of my favorite topics as *no other area in your practice will bring you greater success than what you can accomplish in the final stage of the ATR System: Return.*

Most dentists spend all this money on the attraction phase trying to draw into their office that patient that they have never seen and more importantly a prospect that has never been influenced by their office, or team. *You are really throwing money into an unidentified source!* Instead of spending all this money trying to attract new patients, turn your attention to the patients you already have. Now, I know you are probably thinking that I devoted a lot of time teaching you the importance of getting a body in the chair. It's crucial that you do that, but your success depends upon what you do after you have them in your chair. In fact, what you do will either *grow your practice, keep it the same, or weaken it.*

After the attraction stage is completed, we can add even more value through the treatment planning phase. After planning and completing treatment, what's next? *You must keep your patients returning and referring to your office because this stage alone will be the single greatest contributor to your long-term success.*

It makes much more sense to focus your resources on the patients who have already met you, have been exposed to your team, and have already had a *wow!* experience in your office. Doesn't it make sense that any future business will come from these patients rather than people you haven't yet met? Pamper these patients, send them valuable content, birthday acknowledgments, and appreciation gifts. Don't you think it's easier for someone who has already bought from you to buy again rather than convince someone you've never met to buy from you? Doesn't it make sense to focus on the people who already trust you? Don't try to swim upstream looking for gold. *Most of the time, it's right in your backyard. Returning patients* are *your gold.*

So what is the best and most effective way to accomplish this? First, look at your setup. When patients arrive at your office, figure out the best way to keep in touch and connect with them after they leave their appointment. This requires you and your staff to plan and think ahead. Before they leave, ask for their e-mail, cell phone number, and home address.

Stay in touch with your patients by sending postcards, letters in the mail, making phone calls, and sending appointment reminders online, over the phone, and through regular mail.

My goal for you is to re-invent your practice here. We as dentists have all heard of recall systems and calling the patient to come back in for their cleaning, but *returning* encompasses much more than that. I challenge you to think outside of the box. Out of the myriad of ways to have patients come back into your office, the most effective way is through personal and online communications. Let's first talk about personal communications. This would include phone calls and in-person appointments. Afterward, we will dive into online communications.

You must have a *plan of return* that loops them back to your office after every appointment. Well, how do you do that? Let's review a few scenarios.

Here is the greatest loss of all: a patient comes into your office, spends all that time getting x-rays, getting examined, and listening to what they need to get done. Then, they leave without taking action. What about that *return plan* that loops them back into the office?

This scenario happens all too often. The patient needs $5,000 worth of treatment, and your front office staff schedules the patient for a cleaning in six months. What a way to get them back in the office! This makes me furious! Having your patient come back for a cleaning in six months is not part of the return plan. Instead, the return plan should include getting that patient back into the office for the $5,000 treatment as soon as possible. Ever wonder why dentists have been called *closet millionaires?* It's because they have all this treatment diagnosed and unscheduled sitting idle in their *so called* recall system!

You must have detailed notes in the chart for your patients to remind your staff to call them in one or two weeks after they leave your office if they did not schedule another appointment. Your front and back office staff has to be making these notes based on what you tell them clinically. The more detail you provide, the better their notes, and the more likely they can reconnect with patients and have them come back in. We use Dentrix and place all of our notes in the *office journal* section. The front office staff prints out that journal every month to see which patients have been called and which ones need a follow-up call or email.

For instance, if you saw a patient who needed two crowns because of gross decay on teeth #12 and #13 and no treatment had begun that day or had been scheduled for a later date, it should be annotated in the patient's chart that a follow-up call is needed. Here is the secret though: show your front office staff the x-rays of these patients so they, too, can visualize *why* they need treatment. In the chart, your staff might write, *"Call Mrs. Jones and ask her how her dog's surgery went and also remind her that she needs to get those crowns done because of the cavities she has on those teeth, tell her that the doctor reviewed her x-rays with me and suggested I call."* Once your staff makes contact with the patient in this way, offer the patient an appointment day and time: "I have a 10 a.m. on Wednesday available. Would that work for you?"

This approach works because you are immediately connecting with the patient on something personal and then giving them a reminder to get their treatment done based on a clinical detail that you(the doctor) reviewed with that patient(and front office). A simple, sincere, and personal phone call goes a long way. Suggesting an appointment time works well because you're not asking whether or not they *want* to come in. Instead, you're suggesting a way, an answer, or a *solution* for them to get started. Never ask an open- ended question like, "When do you want to come in to get this done?" Always give them a time so they start to think in terms of a solution to get their treatment done. You might call it manipulation but, in the end, patients really do appreciate you and your office holding their hand and guiding them back to the office to get that necessary treatment done. In their eyes, you care and didn't forget about them, and you made it a priority to follow up.

Your return plan must include the following daily tasks. Ensure that your reception area staff makes these tasks a daily priority, no matter what. (Remember, this is what you should do if the patient did not make another appointment but needs treatment.)

First, have your front office team document a detailed personal and clinical note on the specific treatment your patients need based on their conversations with the patients and your clinical diagnosis. Place this note in a section of your software that can be printed out twice a week showing the patients who need a follow-up within the next month.

Second, call patients back no later than two weeks from the original appointment, and use the personal and clinical information annotated in the chart to reconnect with them. *Remember*-this means they are not just calling and saying, "Mrs. Jones, we saw that you need some treatment done and were wondering if you were ready to schedule for some of that treatment."

Third, suggest an appointment time for treatment. Offer a specific day and time and avoid asking open-ended questions that allow your patients to procrastinate. *Review the details in the "Mastering the Phones" chapter.*

What if they don't need treatment and just need to get a cleaning in six months? All too often, this is where most offices fail. The regular routine here is for patients to fill out a postcard with their contact information so that the staff can send it out in six months. Instead, schedule them on the spot, and tell them that they will get a reminder call and e-mail a week before the appointment to re-confirm. The key here is, even if it's six months from now, get them an appointment before they leave!

Strive to schedule patients for a return visit before they leave their current appointment. If they don't have a future appointment scheduled, your front office staff will have to chase them, which amounts to wasted time and resources.

At this point you might be thinking, *Well, what's the point of getting them into the system if they are going to cancel or reschedule?* To start, this mentally *commits* them for another appointment before they leave your office. It also makes it a lot easier for your staff. Later, we will go into more detail about how to make it easier for you and your team to do this.

In the next section, I am going to show you the most powerful tools that we all have within our reach, at little or no cost to us. We are living in the most technologically advanced time in the history of our civilization. People are communicating in ways that were unheard of just five years ago, and businesses are finding customers and keeping them using these tools. You and your office *must* be set up so your brand can reach your patients. Eric Schmidt, one of the co-founders of Google said, "More content is created every 48 hours than the beginning of time till 2003!" *Wow!* If you think about what that really means, you'll be shocked *and inspired*. It's exciting to know that people are creating content, information, systems, and messages to communicate their thoughts simply because there is an audience out there with an open ear that *wants to listen to them.* Your patients make up a portion of that audience. *You should be inspired to create some of that content for your audience.*

"Where do we start, and what do we do next?" is the question I get all too often from successful doctors with a new or thriving practice. Now that I have introduced you to the return plan, the final stage of the ATR System, let's talk about the best *ways* to get patients to return *and* refer.

Chapter 14

CREATING YOUR OFFICE
BEYOND YOUR LOCATION

Your office is just your location; you must also establish a presence.

Only 26% of small businesses have invested time or effort in marketing online. Yet, nearly all consumers (97 percent) use the Internet to find businesses, products, and services. That means businesses with online marketing strategies are winning.

In order for your patients to return and refer, you must meet them half way. Get to know where they consistently hang out, and interact with them in those places. In essence, you have to create your office outside of your office. *A presence beyond your location is the key to all great business successes.*

What exactly does this mean? Well, we've already established that there are three stages (attraction, treatment planning, and returning) to work through in order to grow your practice. What if I told you that there are tools and strategies out there that can at least activate two out of the three stages above? What if I said that these tools and strategies are inexpensive, easy to learn, and can be outsourced to a team member? What if

I claimed that these tools and strategies make it possible for you to go to where your patients are and provide value to them before they even step into your office? In essence, you would be creating your presence outside of your office. You would be establishing your office beyond your location.

It's all about effectively creating your dental footprint online. If you or your patients are living in modern times, which I hope you are, then you will agree that most of your patients spend a lot of their time online using social networks, e-mail, and video sites. Wouldn't it be smart to go to your patients first and educate them so that they can decide whether or not to come to your office? That is exactly what I mean by *establishing your office beyond your location.* You have the potential to reach patients far beyond your actual office location.

Think of how small of an impact you actually have when your office, your services, and your expertise are contained within the four walls of your dental practice. If you truly understand how this limits your growth, you will have no problem using the new skills, tools, and psychology you'll need to thrive in the new world of dentistry. Welcome to creating a successful online dental presence with thousands of raving fans!

Many dentists boast about their website or their Facebook page. Some may have even tried using Twitter. But having a website doesn't guarantee success in your practice. You must understand that your website, Facebook, YouTube, and Twitter are just tools.

The real value of a website or Facebook page comes only when you understand how to use them in harmony with each other to market your practice and leave a lasting impression on your patients.

Mastering these online tools will benefit your practice because of the extraordinary potential to springboard your office to an entirely different level. I love online marketing for dentistry, and I have successfully marketed my offices and have taught other doctors to do the same for theirs. Master this section and I promise you will watch your practice reach new heights. Remember: your *virtual* presence initiates the attraction and return stages simultaneously.

There's a lot of awesome content here! I am committed to making your office a phenomenal online presence by creating raving fans out of your existing patients and creating new patients by reaching them online. Here,

I'm going to lay out the bare essentials to setup and then show you how all of it should work together. Think of it as if it were a big orchestra playing the best music. You can have all the musicians and instruments, but unless you know how to harmonize it all, you won't have the best music.

Before we go further, take a look at these staggering statistics about what is happening online and with social media. It's a bold reminder as to what is happening to small businesses and how your patient is interacting with you in ways you don't even know. Here are the facts:

- Approximately 7 billion people are on the planet
- 1.8 billion computers worldwide are connected to the Internet
- Over 29.6 million small businesses are in the US (44.6 million if you include home-based businesses)
- There are 950 million active, registered Facebook users
- 1 in 9 people on the planet have a Facebook account (61% of the users are older than 38)
- Over 250 million Twitter accounts exist (64% of Twitter users are over 39)
- 5.6 billion mobile phone accounts are in use worldwide
- A 96% open rate for text messages
- There are over 300 million small businesses worldwide
- When people are searching, Google is now telling them to go to YouTube

As you can see, your online presence and social media are the lifeline for you and your practice.

When I evaluated my own online presence, I could see areas in which we needed improvement. My efforts were scattered because I didn't know how to integrate the different tools and websites out there. I can't count the number of times I've been offered a spot (for a price, of course) on the first page of Google. And I won't deny it; to say that Google is huge would be an understatement, but you must ask yourself if being on the first page is the answer to being *online* with your practice.

Here is what I've found. It's not about being on the first page of Google; rather, it's about your *presence online.* What, exactly, is a presence? When people visit your website, what is it that they see? What about your message? Who are you? Isn't that what they're trying to discover? When I finally understood what our patients need from us online before scheduling their first appointment, I learned that an online presence is a sweet spot that can be recreated using a few key elements. *Think of it in terms of a success triangle for taking your practice online.*

THE ONLINE SUCCESS TRIAD

To create a virtual practice and to be successful online, you have to set up an **Online Presence Triangle®**. Take a look at the picture below.

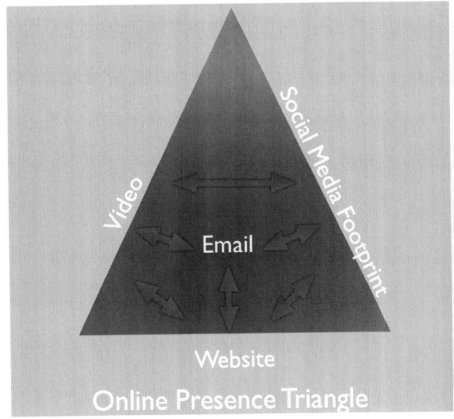

Online Presence Triangle®

Your website is the base of your triangle; video and social media are the sides of it. The concept of e-mail is in the center since having the patient's e-mail is integral for establishing and maintaining the synergy of communication. It is also the central link of communication to your patients after they come into your office. All the arrows in the diagram designate the communication links between the different sides of the triangle. The arrows represent the following:

- Add content-rich video to your website for your current or prospective patients.
- Display your social media footprint via the various links and applications incorporated into your website.
- Use your patients' e-mail to send them to your blog, your social media sites, and your YouTube channel.
- E-mail your patients videos on dental health-related topics and recommend they tell their friends and family to watch as well.
- Embed your videos on Facebook, and e-mail your patients the link to your Facebook page. Also encourage them to "Like" your page.
- Conduct campaigns and value-added promotions on Facebook that drive your existing patient-base back to your office. You can also target a very specific demographic of patients that surround your office through the Facebook Ads feature.

Do you see how all sides of the triangle are connected and how all the online elements are interrelated?

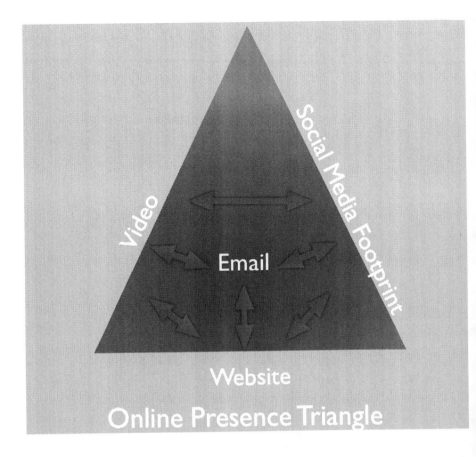

It's not about being on the first page of Google; it's about having a total office presence online. Although your positioning in the Google ranks is important for visibility, Google favorably weighs any quality content that is congruent with your brand. Your prospective patients don't just click and make appointments just because of your positioning on Google. They look around and see if you and your office seem like a place they would feel comfortable visiting. I think you understand the importance of setting up your Online Presence Triangle now! Now, let me show you how you can do this. In the following chapters, we'll take a tactical approach to setting up your online presence as we move through each side of our triangle.

Chapter 15

WHAT'S YOUR E-MAIL?

When you ask your patients for their email, realize that they are giving you a direct link to a communication outlet they keep in their pockets and purses. This is powerful!

E-mail is an extremely powerful and cost-effective way to maintain contact with your patients and add tremendous value. Because it's the quickest and most convenient way to communicate with your patients, it's the focal point of our online presence triangle. People get a ton of junk e-mail every day, but very few of them get e-mails from their dentist. *Most dentists will not personally e-mail their patients with useful and interesting information.* What I'm talking about is different from an e-mail newsletter; it's a personal e-mail to each and every one of your patients, similar to something you would send a friend. Just make sure it's still professional and not something like, "Yo. Wassup."

It sounds really simple, but some practices make it hard on themselves. Move away from the old way of thinking that you have to send out postcards, phone call reminders, and letters in the mail. In the previous chapter we spoke about calling your patients back for treatment, but you could also e-mail them valuable, content-driven e-mail pieces that detail treatment options. Remember the goal is to educate them so that they see the value in committing to their treatment. Tell your front office staff that your goal is to communicate with your patients online, that their e-mail is even more important than getting their home address. Some office managers and treatment coordinators ask for e-mail so that they can send patients special promotions and offers. Don't make that mistake! No one wants another special offer from your office; what patients really want is informative, content-driven places they can go, places that help *them*. Your content, in some way, form, or another, must be useful for specific patients. Remember, marketing means consistently adding massive value.

4 WAYS TO CAPTURE YOUR PATIENTS' E-MAIL ADDRESSES

1. **Emphasize that you must enter them in your automated system** so that you never *forget about their recall cleaning visits* and, this way, a reminder will go out to them every three or six months. Point out that you won't be sending a ton of e-mails, only specific ones for their appointments.

2. **It's for their convenience, so that they can schedule their appointments online,** get a reminder for an appointment, and confirm their appointment without having to call the office. Patients love this type of convenience, so show them that your office has the technology to give them a more *convenient* means of communication. Every time we present it like this, patients are actually happy that we won't be calling them; instead, they can rely on a quick e-mail correspondence to remind and confirm their appointment. Software, such as Demandforce, can do this for you and even automate it! We will discuss this in a later chapter but, to put it succinctly, it is an *automatic* system that makes it easier for your patients to return to your office with less effort and time spent on painstaking administrative tasks. More on that later.

3. *Always* suggest that patients schedule their next appointment before leaving your office *even if* it's six months from now. This eliminates the wasted effort spent getting them back in for their recall via traditional methods. I went over this earlier, but I can't stress enough the importance of this. When you make this suggestion, also tell them they can reschedule their appointment online through a click of a button if they need to. This is a huge key in getting them scheduled this early. Let your patients know this can be done only if you have their e-mail address. This way, patients don't feel the burden of commitment for an appointment six months prior. Look at it as a *risk eliminator* so they actually take the initiative and schedule the appointment. You'll see, when patients get an appointment reminder online, they'll usually make it to that appointment.

4. **Let them know that your office has specials exclusive to your online patient** *community.* This is important. Inform patients that your office has an online community. Don't just say that they will get an e-mail from you! Patients should feel that this *community* is designed for *their* convenience and will be valuable to *them*.

E-mail your patients, for example, that it was great having them in your office and that it was wonderful seeing them the other day. Also tell them that you posted a new article on your blog, and give them the link to go check it out. On your blog, post some informative content on anything of interest or value to their health. I am limiting it to the topic of health, at this point, since you are their dentist, and before you start posting anything on other topics, you must first be interested in adding value to their well-being.

You must position yourself as the expert in *health & dentistry* and not just teeth. Whether you like it our not, your patients already see you in this light anyway, so you might as well start from there and then diversify your topics if you wish. If you want more information on how your oral health is connected to your overall systemic health, the articles in most dental journals outline this connection. *When you blog about a particular topic, go beyond just teeth; it increases value.* We will go over some catchy topics for articles, blog posts, and videos in a later chapter.

When your patients go to your blog, they are there to learn. Most blogs don't aim to hard sell and are informative in purpose. So, what types of content can you post on your blog? You can post anything, such as a blurb about an e-book that you wrote, articles written by you or someone else, videos, or even an interesting report, like the "Top Five Keys to Whiter Teeth." Give them something of value, something they want to read. They're not interested in why your office is better then anyone else's. Who cares? Don't get me wrong here. It's important for patients to understand what separates you from the rest of the practices but, more often, patients want information that is directly *useful* and *applicable* to them.

You could even e-mail your patients about an interesting video on your Facebook page and suggest they watch because it lists food to avoid because they cause bad breath. With their e-mail address, you can direct them to any medium you choose. This gives you immediate control of how you represent your brand.

With e-mail, you can direct your prospective patients and, more importantly, your current ones, where you want them to go. E-mail should be part of your *return plan*. For new patients you haven't seen yet, focus on answering any questions they may have about dental health, their kids' teeth, or any anything else. You can stay in touch with your patients (both current and prospective) by the new videos, articles, and content pieces you send them via e-mail. Now, let's talk about a place we call home: your website.

Chapter 16

CREATING YOUR WEBSITE

When someone comes to your home, focus on them,
remember them, and then call them back.

hen I was young, my parents always had people over at the house. I couldn't understand why, but it was so important for my parents to *feed* them and make sure some sort of feast was ready for them when they arrived. This was especially true if they were coming over for the first time. The house had to be clean, and the food and drinks had to be ready to serve. I always wished they would come over, hang out, and then leave.

Eventually, I grew out of that naïve way of thinking and understood that when someone comes to you, whether to your practice or to your website, you must serve them and give them focus, importance, and cater to them with *value*.

I want you to look at your website no differently. It is the base of the online presence triangle and where your patients are landing when they see you online. But what do most offices do? They boast to their patients about their accomplishments, their fancy equipment, and education. What if you did that when people came to your home? I doubt they would come back!

A majority of dental practices are missing the mark when it comes to creating a strong *value-adding* website. Most dental practice websites are like a big fancy banner. No one wants to see another banner site about how great your office is. Instead, it should *feed* your patients with value and messages that they can take away and feel comfortable about when they leave. I think this is a powerful analogy that relays the importance of giving away something of value to anyone that enters your domain or home.

Your website is a place patients can learn more about what *they* want, not who you are.

Now that we have refreshed our perspective about the concept of a website, let's view it within the context of our online presence triangle. You now understand that you *need* a website; it is the base of our online presence triangle, and it interacts with the social media and video elements we talked about earlier. But what do you put *on* your website, and what should your website *do* for your patients?

TOP 5 THINGS YOUR WEBSITE SHOULD DO FOR YOUR PATIENTS

1. It *immediately* gives away something of value to your visitors.
2. It allows you to capture your patients' information(current or prospective) and interact with them.
3. It shows a video on your office and information/tabs on all the services you provide along with office hours.
4. It allows patients to schedule appointments online.
5. It has authentic and raw *video testimonials* for every procedure you do at your office.

These are elements that you must have on your website. You could also include some before and after photos of all those nice veneers cases you did, but even those should be integrated with what is listed above. For example, if you include a before and after photo, put it under the video testimonial on the veneers you just finished with that particular patient. Before and after pictures are a dime a dozen, and no one really knows if you just grabbed them online somewhere, but video testimonials are genuine and more personal. Let's review the purpose of your website in more detail.

1. It *immediately* gives away something of value to your visitors.

I used the word *immediately* because these items should be given away as soon as someone visits your site. This doesn't include a drawing that they have to enter or a contest. Be sincere about this. The best item to give away is an *informational product.* It can be in the form of an e-book, DVD, or a video link. We will talk more about the power of video, but nothing else comes as close to a strong message as videos on your site.

TOPIC IDEAS

- You can write an e-book called The Best Over-the-Counter Products for your Teeth. It can be a simple five-page e-book that reviews these products. Supermarkets sell a slew of dental products that people have no idea how to use. Information like this truly adds value and educates your prospective patients.
- Draft an article titled, "The Top Three Ways to Prevent Cavities (It's Not What You Think!)." My own ideas for articles have come from reading dental magazines and research studies. When summarized and translated, it's tremendously useful for your patients. Sharing an article like this would establish your expert status within your community. You want people to see you as the go-to dentist.
- Create a video on "How to Properly Floss in Two Minutes." Make this a video link you send to them via e-mail. Be raw and be real with your patients, and they will come back to you for more videos.
- Write about something cool and unique that only your office does.
- Offer a free, take-home bleaching tray. Because many offices use this approach, try to be different. For example, if you give away a kit, also include an e-book.

Do you get the concept? Remember how we said earlier that even in the online world you must first give and then receive? Considering that your website is your patients' first form of contact, wouldn't it be great to get a gift from you as a token of the beginning of a long-term relationship? Assume you will be their dentist! Remember, it's critical that you give to your patients something they really *want*.

As important as it is to give away the cool stuff, it's more important that you don't give them useless stuff. Here are *low-value* items, or information, that you should never give away:

- Why your office is the best and better than anyone else's. You can have this on your site somewhere, but don't promote it because it doesn't *give* anything to your patients.
- All the accolades you have received. Note: If you are a celebrity dentist or an icon in the field, this would be helpful to have on your site but it's *not* something you can give away. In this case, have video testimonials from your celebrity clients; but don't use them as a value product to give away.
- All your high-tech gadgets. If you give something like this away, tie it into a report like, "How to get your crown done in one visit with no temporaries." But also realize that this content will exclude people who don't think they need a crown. More people want to know about "whitening secrets" than crown and bridge work. Let's not forget that when patients come in for their whitening, you can educate them about the crown they need.

2. It allows you to capture your patients' information(current or prospective) and interact with them.

This is the most critical feature of your website! Don't be confused. You can give away valuable free content, but give it in exchange for their *name* and *e-mail*. A webform, which is one of the ways your website grabs e-mail addresses, is one way to accomplish this. In internet marketing terms, it's called an *opt-in* page. A webform is simple to place on your site, and your webmaster can do this in a matter of minutes. Doing this opens the line of communication with your prospective patients.

The next step is to *drip feed* them interesting and valuable content every few weeks. Where will you post all of this amazing content? On your social media footprint, such as your blog, your Facebook page, your Twitter page, or even on your YouTube channel.

You're probably thinking, *Geez, this is a lot of work* or *I don't have time to post all this stuff all day when I am focusing on Mr. Jones's RCT or Janet's crown and bridge.* The good news is that all of this can be automatized, but first, spend some time setting up camp and knowing your vision for your practice.

All of this can be accomplished using *autoresponders*. An autoresponder sets up a series of e-mails, videos, or articles that go out to a targeted list of people that you acquired through a webform or another list. For instance, if you captured their name and e-mail from the information they entered on your website, all of those e-mails will go directly into an *autoresponder campaign*. A campaign is a pre-created, value-packed sequence of e-mails that are set to go out to your list. Some of these e-mails would have links to videos you posted on your YouTube page or even helpful articles on your practice's blog. In a nutshell, you are engaging with your patients and visitors on your site. This interactivity establishes your practice as the *source* of dental health information in the community.

Here are the internet marketing industry standards for effective autoresponders:

Aweber at www.aweber.com is an excellent service, is easy to use, and it's inexpensive. The downside is that if you are importing your patients from your dental software database, such as Dentrix or Eaglesoft, you're required to have all of your e-mail addresses opt-in and confirm that it's okay to e-mail them. I don't like this because your patients, who have already given you their information, might be wondering why they need to tell you again that they want to be e-mailed.

iContact at www.icontact.com is easy to use, is inexpensive and, with over 600,000 users worldwide, it does *not* require you to have your e-mail addresses opt-in to in order to email them.

Infusionsoft at www.infusionsoft.com has a big learning curve, it's more expensive, but it's very robust. You can check out this one, but I recommend the ones above. Infusionsoft is ideal if you have a shopping cart on your website, but chances are you won't.

Make sure you download all of the e-mails from your dental software and import them into one of the above systems. This will enable you to send your content to your existing patients without them having to fill out a webform on your website.

Between the prospective patients coming to your site and the ones you already have, you should really be able to keep everyone you know engaged with valuable content about dental health and other relevant topics.

3. It shows a video about your office and information/tabs on all of the services you provide along with office hours.

When people search for a dentist and land on your website, they are *not* looking to find out more about your Super Dentist status and what you can do for their teeth. Patients first want to know whether or not they can *trust you.* Second, what is your office like? Is it clean and safe? Is it also fun and happy? Make sure your office atmosphere is communicated in your website. That's why I suggest placing a video on the first page of your site. Using videos is one of the most powerful ways to build that *initial trust* in a matter of seconds.

Let's use my site as an example. Go to www.socalsmiles.net. As soon as someone lands on the site, the first thing that happens is a video plays immediately. Have your video set to play as soon as someone lands on your page. Research shows that many times, when you do have a video up, most people won't click *play.* Setting your video to auto-play optimizes your video for Google and YouTube as you get more views.

What about trust? Like we said before, you need to build trust immediately. The video that is playing gives your visitors instant access to your world, your practice, and your team. The content of your video should cast a positive light on your office and team in a fun and creative manner; this will give your visitors a *feel* of your office. Most people are already apprehensive about seeing their dentist, but this draws them into your dental world and helps calm their anxiety. All it takes is a simple video to give your visitors two of the most influential elements —that of *trust* and *feel.*

What kind of video should you upload? You want to post videos that are creative, authentic, and show personality. You do not want videos that cost thousands of dollars to make! Make it raw and authentic. What's the biggest video site in the world today? YouTube, of course, and what do they have on their site? Raw, authentic, and personality-driven videos! This sells, and this is what people want to see. Nobody wants another picture-perfect commercial; we use TiVo and DVRs to skip over those commercials. People like watching what is real. If you want a good crash course on the significance of authentic content on your site, read *Crush It!* by Gary Vaynerchuk. He talks about how authentic video is dominating the marketplace in every industry since people are more and more inclined for *truth-based, value-added marketing.* Don't worry about what's behind you, or if you have patients in the office, or even if you forgot to say something and you stumbled. People like to see that! Be real! No one wants boring and scripted.

Here are some video content ideas for your homepage:

- An office tour with pictures of your office and staff. You can place small titles or descriptions of your team. This can easily be made from home on iMovie using your MacBook.
- A meet-the-team video where you talk to every person on your team for ten seconds. They each share something small they've learned about dental health and taking care of your teeth.
- Patient testimonials about you, the dentist, and your team. Imagine landing on a website and watching patients deliver unscripted testimonials, right on the front page, talking about their dentist: *you!* This is powerful!
- A dental tip of the month. You could record twelve simple tips for your patients every month and place the video on your site. Obviously, they would not have to opt-in for these tips as there would be one tip a month automatically on your site. On the flip side, these same video tips can be used to get their e-mail and send

them a tip a month. For this, they would have to opt-in (on the homepage) to receive these e-mails.

TABS FOR YOUR SERVICES

Also make sure you have specific tabs for your services that patients can click on. These tabs should not be hard to find when visitors land on your homepage. If you go back to my website again, you'll see a tab for our services; it's just one tab and it explains everything we do. Clicking on the tab takes you to a page with all the dental services we offer and video testimonials for each of those services. Keep it clean and simple. With one click, patients are where you want them to be.

I think you get the overall idea here. It's actually really simple when you think about it from the patient's point of view. What do they want to see? What would make them browse around more and stay on your website long enough to make an appointment? The simple answer here is *value*. Create a value-based site that focuses on what your practice can *give them*. What can your practice do to better them, to be of more interest to them? Think of your patient first and then your office. If you create enough value for them for simply visiting your website and they still don't make an appointment, you might be able to keep in touch with them via e-mail if they opted in for something you were offering. As long as you have an e-mail address, you can continually communicate through a pre-created e-mail sequence that eventually leads them into your office.

4. It allows patients to schedule appointments online.

Your patients need to get into your office in the most efficient and most *convenient* way possible. The most effective way is through an online appointment! Let me roll this one out for you. Patients make an online appointment through your website indicating the exact time (in thirty-minute increments) and date they wish to come in. As soon as they hit the submit button, an e-mail is sent to them indicating that your office has received their appointment *request* and that you will be in touch with them shortly. At the same time, your team gets an e-mail saying that an appointment request has been made with the necessary important patient contact details, their health forms, and so on. That's it.

Let me clarify something about online appointment requests. They are just requests and are open for modification based on your schedule. Patients understand this and don't expect that when they send in an appointment request online, you will always be able to grant them that exact time for their appointment. They expect a call back or a confirmation, and this is the value of online appointments.

This opens up a new opportunity for efficiency and productivity within your team. An online appointment *request* is so much more time-effective than a phone call, which interrupts other important tasks. It's not easy when you're trying to bill out insurance or prepare for a treatment plan, and you're interrupted by a phone call from a new patient who probably has many questions about the office and requires more of your time and energy than you're able to give. The online appointment request,brings the element of organizing your time back to you. Now, your front office staff can call back that appointment request when he or she is fully prepared and 100% present. You are in control again. Our office policy states that the front office team should respond to all morning appointment requests by the afternoon and call them all back by then. All those patients that submitted online appointment requests in the afternoon get call backs in the evening by 6 p.m. that same day.

Your website should have multiple online request appointment buttons. In fact, I have an appointment request button on every single page of the site. It's not overbearing; it's simply easy to find. This way, we take appointment requests twenty-four hours a day and seven days a week, including the days we are closed. It's a great feeling seeing an appointment request in your inbox on a day or time that the office is closed. It's a neat reminder of how your office presence is still working while you are not! See how your online presence lives beyond your office?

Here is the *essential information* you must request from patients in order to accept online appointments on your website or blog. You can give this list to your webmaster so he or she can properly set up your appointment page.

ONLINE APPOINTMENT REQUEST FORMS SHOULD INCLUDE THE FOLLOWING:

First Name

Last Name

E-mail

Phone

What can we help you with? Provide a dropdown menu here with common procedures offered at your office. Include exams and x-rays here as well.

Make an appointment with a calendar pop-up.

What time Provide a dropdown menu of times in thirty-minute increments.

Promotion box for patients to enter any promotion codes.

How did you hear about us? Ah, the golden question. It's important to track your patient-base, so keep this box open for patients to type in the names of any online sources. When your patients come to your office, indicate in their chart the source of referral.

Comments This should also be an open box where patients can enter specific comments. Many times patients express that one of their teeth has been hurting or they cracked a filling, and they need to come in as soon as possible.

You can always add more, but these are the essential items you'll want to include. The information your patients provide here will give you an idea of their needs and preferences. On average, we get about three to five appointment requests a day through online appointment requests. Our goal is to make the majority of our appointments originate online. Make it your goal, too.

5. It has authentic and raw video testimonials for every procedure you do at your office.

This is an absolute genius idea. We will take a meticulous look at the power of video in the next chapter but, for now, I'm going to introduce you to the best way to get testimonials. How many dental websites have you been to where there are written testimonials from their patients, signed off with their initials? Now, how many websites have you been to where there were authentic video testimonials of patients who just finished treatment? The answer: very likely none or just a few. This type of information is so powerful for patients making treatment decisions, and even choosing a dentist. It hits both stages of our ATR mind-set, the attraction and return stage, since patients who are considering a particular type of treatment can hear from someone else who has already done it. *Your goal is to have a video testimonial on your website for **every treatment that you offer**.* For instance, when your patients click on *Services*, they should also see a video testimonial from a real patient of yours who had that same treatment. This is what is called *social proof*, and we will learn more about it in the next few chapters.

Let's take a comprehensive look at what you need to do to make video technology work for you!

Chapter 17

THE POWER OF VIDEO

A picture is worth a thousand words, but a video shows a great story!

Video is the way of the future, and the future in engaging with your patients is being created right now as you read this page. Video will be a large and influential part of how you and I view the world, learn the things we need to know, get the information we desire and, most importantly, communicate to our patients when we are not around them. If you don't believe me, just stop and really think about how many videos are generated every minute. Sixty hours of video is uploaded on YouTube every single *minute*. Now that's just YouTube; there are countless other sites out there uploading videos in an attempt to spread their message and share information.

Still not convinced? It's hard not to be when the evidence is so blazingly obvious. The shift in how our patients make purchases and the research on where they're spending their money is more and more being influenced by the *art of video*. With all the excitement about spreading our message through online videos, we can become sidetracked on what content we should focus our attention on. The bottom line is that the use of videos should be a large part of marketing your office.

When we start talking about *how* to do video, most people still get a lost and confused look on their face because they don't have big movie production studios in their homes or offices. But you don't need to know much about shooting videos or even editing for that matter. A simple handheld video camera is all you need, and it usually costs under $200. Using the power of a $200 handheld video camera you can shoot high definition video that looks professional. You simply plug it into your computer, load it onto one of the popular video editing software, such as iMovie or Sony Vegas, and you've got yourself a *great storytelling medium with which to market your office*. Don't overestimate the effort needed here, and don't underplay its value. Video converts your viewers to fans and patients faster than anything you can type on your site about dentistry!

We have learned that marketing equals consistently adding massive value. Where can we add value to our patients and those that are yet to come into our office? **We should structure our videos and content effectively so the layout of the videos enhances our marketability and the content adds great value.** Here are the main layout and content areas you should focus on to be successful at making videos geared toward your patient-base.

THE 5 CONTENT AREAS FOR YOUR VIDEOS

1. **A personalized office tour:** Don't do a tour with one of those lame 360° camera angles. Take a tour using still pictures with simple transitions between them, and throw in some music. Or, hold your camera and tour your office introducing and interviewing your team. Make it about two to three minutes, and that's it!

2. **A comical video on teeth and dentistry:** Shoot a comical video on something you did in your office. Ever notice how some of the dumbest and pointless videos are also the ones out there that receive the most traffic? People always like humor, so use it to your advantage.

3. **An informational video with personality:** Shoot a short informational video with you talking about something your patients always ask about. Make it fun and interesting. Remember to keep it raw and authentic, and don't be afraid to show your personality and uniqueness.

Here are some topics that you can put on video with a little bit of research and time:

- Top foods for your teeth
- Healthy vitamins for your teeth and gums
- Five over-the-counter dental products to use
- The top all natural dental products
- Everything you need to know about Zoom teeth whitening
- Everything you need to know about Invisalign
- The best thing about cosmetic dentistry
- Causes of bad breath
- The hidden secrets of cosmetic dentistry
- The one thing they don't tell you about teeth whitening
- The ten things you must know before going to the dentist
- How to overcome bad breath
- An advanced technology or technique used in your office to elevate your patients' experience

These are all about the topics your patients may be interested in. You can also turn these videos into nicely written articles as well.

4. **Video testimonials:** Again, video testimonials on a dental website are unique and powerful examples of the quality of service your patients can expect from you. How do we shoot these testimonials? Many dentists think that shooting these is an arduous task when, in actuality, it's quite simple and takes no more than two minutes per person. To shoot great testimonials, let's ask ourselves what we really need from an exceptional testimonial. Remember the three most important things your testimonial should capture?

It has to be raw, authentic, and show personality. In this case, it's the patient who has to have some personality. You shouldn't call your patients in for a video testimonial a day or two after the procedure when their hair and make-up are perfect. Remember, we're not shooting a commercial. If you went to a dental appointment with a friend and waited for him chairside to get the gist of his treatment experience, wouldn't you get the *real*, unedited version of the experience since you'd get to ask him about it immediately after his appointment? You may say, "Hey, how did it go, I'm going in next week?" That is the same thing you must do with your patient, ask them right after the treatment. It may go something like this:

> **Dentist:** You're all done, John!
>
> **Patient:** Perfect. Thanks. That wasn't too bad at all.
>
> **Dentist:** John, Can I ask you for a quick favor? If you really had a positive experience with us and feel comfortable enough, would you mind saying a few words—no more than twenty seconds—on my little handheld camera? We put these videos on our website to help other patients feel comfortable about procedures they might be nervous about. You'd be doing them a great service because it really helps them feel more comfortable when they watch it.
>
> **Patient:** Sure doc, that's fine…What do you want me to say? I'm not that great of a speaker, but I will do my best.
>
> **Dentist:** Thanks! You don't have to be a good speaker, just be yourself. The more real you are, the better it is for others. It's a quick twenty seconds, and I'll walk you through it. Just talk about your experience and mention our office name anytime during your message. Say whatever it is you want to say, even if some parts of your experience were tougher than others.
>
> **Patient:** Okay, that sounds easy enough.

It's that simple. These testimonials should not take long at all. The less time you take on the set-up, the less apprehensive your patients will be. Don't make it a big deal; keep it casual and stress-free. Most importantly, record the video right after the appointment while the patient is still in the dental chair. Remember, *raw and authentic*.

5. **Frequently asked and should-ask questions:** I saved this area till the end because this is the one that I feel is the ***most effective*** way to get inside your patients' minds, and stay there. *If you shoot only one set of videos, then let it be these because, by doing so, you'll distinguish yourself from every other dentist in your city.*

    The FAQ video series is one of the most valuable marketing techniques you can employ. It's marketing at its finest. Throughout the book we have created a paradigm shift in what marketing really is by saying that marketing equals consistently adding massive value. If there was one marketing technique that can be packaged into a bundle, one that exemplifies consistent value creation for your patients, then this is it. It's simple; here's how it works. Think of ten questions your patients always ask you and create a one to three minute video addressing each. These are your frequently asked questions. *Each question is a separate video.* It can be something like, "What is the best toothpaste to use?" Another one could be, "Why do my gums bleed when I brush?" Even better, "How can I eliminate bad breath?" Sit down and brainstorm some questions your patients always ask you, then write them down and get started! Shoot ten FAQ videos with answers and also ten should-ask question videos. Should-ask questions are ones like, "What does it *mean* when my gums bleed?" Another might be, "What are the main things that *cause* bad breath?" Think about the should-ask questions in terms of questions you wished they would ask you.

    A patient may ask about the quickest way to straighten their teeth. You can tell them veneers, but a should-ask question would be, "What's the *difference* between veneers and braces when straightening your teeth?" One answer: For veneers, the dentist has to prep the teeth and remove tooth structure, so there may be a limit in the amount of cosmetic straightening that can be done. On the other hand, braces would actually translate the teeth to another position and move the body of the tooth.

    Do you see how the should-ask question is a better question asked by someone with more of an insight to the topic? This is exactly what you as the dentist are doing when you write down your should-ask questions, and make a video for those as well. Don't get too bogged down with the details of the definition; just realize that it's a small distinction that casts a different perspective on the questions that you *should* be getting asked.

What can you do with these twenty mini-videos you just made? If you look at our Online Presence Triangle, you can see that among the many arrows, there are some that go from video to e-mail and also from website to video.

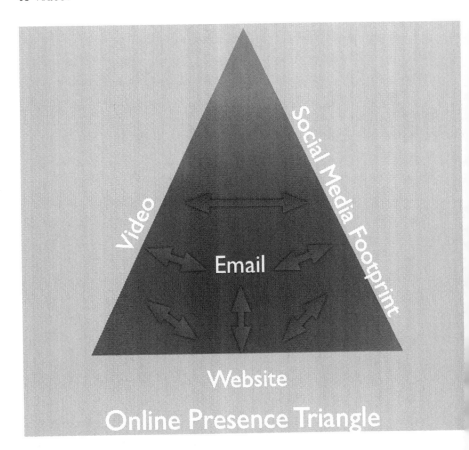

We can place a webform on our website that captures the names and e-mails of prospective patients in return for some free videos on the "Top

10 Questions You've Always Wanted to Ask your Dentist." These are the FAQs. On your blog or website, you can have a place for them to enter their name and e-mail for "10 Teeth-Saving Insights your Dentist Wants to Share with You." These can be the should-ask questions. Do you see what's going on here? You are requesting their name and e-mail, and in return you are giving them some valuable content that improves their dental health and oral awareness. You can deliver these videos via one of the automated e-mail services we discussed earlier. This would mean that as soon as they entered their name and e-mail, your automated service would be set to send out a link to one of these videos, say once a week or every few weeks. It can be a link to your video set in a private area of your blog or website for those who gave their information to you. In essence, you are constantly keeping on *top of mind* and becoming the expert dentist in your area. When patients watch you on video over and over, giving away helpful and interesting content about dental health, nutrition, and lifestyle, they will feel as if they know you very well. You're building trust before those prospective patients even step foot in your office!

When I started creating videos, people were really appreciative. They liked that I actually shot a quick video for *them* and gave them some cool and informative content. Some of my patients come in and tell me they saw my videos on Facebook or YouTube and think it's great that I am doing that. Vendors also have approached me to pitch their products as well. Even though you may not have an interest in dealing with dental vendors, the greater point is that it gets your brand out there and creates opportunity where you may not have seen it before.

You've shot all these videos? Now what? You've got to know where to place them. We have already reviewed what you can do with the twenty frequently asked and should-ask questions, but what about the other ones? Let's keep this simple. A great place to post your videos is Facebook, your website, and your blog.

Put your video testimonials on your website under *Services*. When a visitor clicks on Services, they'll be taken to a list of all the services you offer with video testimonials for each and every one of them. How much better would that be? For every service you have, there is a patient talking about his or her experience on that one service alone. Do you think people are likely to watch a testimonial when they go to your website? Of course they would! You can check out http://www.socalsmiles.net to see what my site looks like with a setup like this already in play.

In addition, remember that you can release these videos to your fanbase on Facebook. Try a weekly video release. We will talk more about the Facebook powerhouse in a later chapter. Now that you have a thorough understanding of what you should put in your videos and the importance of using them to build your office, let's focus on what videos provide: social proof.

Chapter 18

SOCIAL PROOF

There is no greater truth than that of social proof.

You've learned the types of videos to create, the different topics you can talk about, and how to use the videos to get patients' names and e-mail address so that you can keep in touch with them. What about social media? Can you put content, articles, and even videos onto your social media platform? We know that the Online Presence Triangle is made up of three essential elements: the base being your website, one side video, and your other side your social media footprint. So now, let's learn about your social media footprint and how video relates to this. Let's talk about one of the biggest social revolutions we are all witnessing on a daily basis. I know you and your practice have been affected by this in some way. Throw away that newspaper clipping, the yellow pages, that expensive brochure you sent to the new homeowner that just moved into your area, and forget about putting up that big red sign in front of your door that says you're a *Dentist*! All of these modes of marketing have dramatically lost their value. *Welcome to the world of social proof.*

How many times have you asked your friends or family for particular service or product? This is human nature, and today social media harnesses the power of this innate nature of ours. We are wired this way. Social media is like word of mouth on steroids! You as a dentist have the one of the biggest opportunities to capture *this* and then market *that*! I always have people tell me that they saw the videos or testimonials on crowns, or Invisalign on our website, and it made them feel comfortable to see videos of someone else who had done it before them. More so, it gave them insightful information on a procedure they were considering getting done. This is so powerful and patients love it. It's like being able to tell your friend about your services, except now you have the ability to express that to everyone that comes into contact with your online presence. Dentistry is like no other business in the world. Most businesses have a revolving door element to them, where most consumers don't mind going to another place of service or goods if they get a better price or better customer service. It's the one-in and one-out mentality. Dentists, on the other hand, are very different. Most people just don't feel comfortable switching dentists.

Instead, they look for referrals, they ask their friends, they seek direction from their co-workers, and validate all this by looking you up online!

The bottom line is that dentistry is a referral-based business. Haven't you heard of dental offices being around for like thirty years with no marketing whatsoever? How do they survive? The answer is that everyone knew of them and told other people through the years. Then, those people referred other people through the years, and so forth. Thus, dentistry is driven by referrals. This is great news since we are now living in an age of *word of mouth* on *steroids*!

There is no better time to be a dentist because the number one way that patients come to your office is through referrals. Today, we happen to have the coolest, most effective, and easy-to-access referral system ever: social media.

Your patients are on social platforms, and they are looking for the services that you offer. So what's the problem? Most dentists don't have their footprints in the sand leading their patients to their office. Understanding this and implementing it at even a basic level will breed you success online. A good example of this is the use of video testimonials, which we reviewed in the last chapter. When you have an area where prospective patients can instantly see actual video testimonials of patients who have gotten the procedures done that they themselves are interested in, it instantly builds more trust. There are some fundamental truths and setup secrets you must know to harness the power of social media for dentistry. You must set-up...

YOUR SOCIAL MEDIA FOOTPRINT

Why do I call it a *footprint*? Look at your footprint; it's the trail that your brand carves out as it moves ahead online. All these footprints lead to your office. They all lead to your brand and your team. If your footprints are everywhere and are random, with no direction, you will not get any followers or patients coming to your office.

Most dentists don't have their social media footprint set up effectively. They dabble in social media, a little bit of Facebook, some Twitter, think YouTube is for kids, and try out a handful of other sites since they think it's what they're supposed to be doing. That's not a footprint; it's scrambling to write a message that gets muffled and, in the end, no one can understand who you are or what you're trying to say.

In this section, I am going to show you how to set up your Social Media Footprint so that your brand can lead patients to your office, even while you sleep. *Even while you sleep*—I LOVE that part. It's so nice to wakeup and see online appointment request e-mails to me and my team about how they need to come in for their exam or their dental treatment that they finally want to get done. Even if you get one online appointment a day for a twenty-day month, that's an extra twenty patients. Couldn't you use an extra 20 patients in your practice? Let's set you up for online success!

Here is what you will need to set up your Social Media Footprint: *Google Places, Facebook, YouTube, WordPress Blog, and Twitter.* I am going to dive deep into each of these and talk about what they mean for your office, what's involved in the setup, and how you should position yourself in each area.

Chapter 19

GOOGLE PLACES- WHAT'S YOUR ADDRESS?

*Your address is beyond where you live; ideally,
it's everywhere that someone wants you to be.*

Having a physical address puts you on the map or radar, but Google Places opens the door to all the people who see you on that map. Google Places is a feature with Google Maps.

Before we get into Google Maps, let me go over what you see when you search for something on the biggest search engine in the world. Google search is becoming more and more social, and you will start seeing relevant content from Facebook and even Twitter show up on some local searches. I have already noticed some content that I posted on Facebook show up in a Google search. Keep in mind that this was not the case before the introduction of these social media platforms. So, it would make sense that if your practice information is showing up in Google's search results, then you really should establish and claim your business on Google. Claiming your business listing on Google is of great importance since it gives Google your business identity. How do you do that?

Once you have your domain name registered and your website up for a few months, Google will recognize that domain when you type your exact business name in their search box. Look at the search results and find your business. Next to your listing you'll see a blue link that says *Place Page*. Click on this, and it will take you to your Google Places listing. Since you have not verified or claimed your Google Places page, it will say *edit this place-business owner?* Click on that, and open a Google account to fill in all of your necessary business information, and include the necessary pictures, captions, and videos. Make sure you fill out a thorough ad. If you want to have an ongoing promotion that people can see when they land on your Google Places page, you can enter that information in there as well.

It is really important that you post relevant pictures of your office and fill in *all* of the areas that ask you to provide information. When you click on *edit this place* after you have claimed your page, click on *creating a great listing*, review it, and follow Google's instructions. Here are some critical parts of your page that you should have populated:

- Office name (If you have a DBA, put it up!)
- Office address
- Website
- E-mail (Enter an e-mail address that goes to you and your front office staff; don't enter your personal e-mail address.)
- Business hours
- Categories (If you're an orthodontist, recognize that here. If you have other specialists come to your office, then mention that as well.)
- Office pictures and video (Upload some professional pictures of your office. Google owns YouTube, so my suggestion is to place your YouTube office tour here as well.)

After you've set up your Google Places page, Google Maps will mail you a password to access and verify your listing. Once you enter your password, your listing will show as an owner-verified listing.

When people visit your page, they know that the owner has actually claimed this business, and it's legitimate information. One of the most important aspects of this page is that it also holds certified reviews from Google. Patients can write a review directly on your Places page. Depending on Google's ever-changing algorithms, at times, you may even see reviews from third party sites such as Yelp and Demandforce affiliated with your page. The more reviews you have posted, the better optimized or findable your site will be in the search results.

Note- *as of publishing this book Google has since integrated Google Places into their new platform called Google+ Local. Essentially, you still need to do the same thing listed in this chapter starting with finding your Google listing as indicated here, and then clicking on "reviews" and then claiming that listing by opening up a new gmail account OR using one of your existing gmail accounts. As another option you can also click on "Join Google +" once you find your listing. Once you have logged into Google+ using your gmail you can claim this listing and populate it according to what I have discussed here. This is what Google now calls a business page. Just get the process started, it's easy once you find your listing, as there are many links that lead you to the place of getting a Google+ Local profile going. Go for it and you'll see!*

Chapter 20

FACEBOOK FOR DENTISTS

It's the third largest country in the world, and you can visit without a passport; all you need is just a laptop and an internet connection.

In 2005 Facebook had only 2.7 million people! Then, five years later, they had 600 million members! Insane growth! Now, everyone and their grandmother knows about Facebook. According to a report from Experian, it was America's most-visited website in 2010. If Facebook were a country, it would be the third largest country in the world. Do you think that any of your patients are interacting on Facebook? Do you think that they hang out there regularly? You'd better believe they do, and Facebook is here to stay, at least for a while. Here are some more amazing facts about this social media powerhouse:

- Facebook has 950 million active users at the time of writing this book.
- 1 in 7 people on the planet have a Facebook account.
- At least 50 percent of active users log on to Facebook regularly.
- Has their users spending 700 *billion* minutes a month on their site.
- Nearly two-thirds of the U.S. population has a Facebook account.

- Has more page views than 99+ of its competitive sites.
- Accounts for 25 percent of the page views in all of the US page views on the Internet. This fact alone is astounding considering so many people in the United States are online. In other words, 25 percent of the pages that are looked at online are Facebook pages!

These facts have will have changed by the time you read this! The bottom line is that using Facebook is a skill you *must* master! It is as important as keeping up with the most current dental standards and procedures and managing your office. Facebook is a great place for you to add even more value to your patients' lives.

The setup: If you don't already have a Facebook profile, go to www.facebook.com and start your own personal profile page. After filling out your personal profile page, you should start your Facebook business page. You must have your profile page set up first to start your business page. Business pages are called *Pages*, and personal profile pages are called *Profiles*. Don't worry; your personal *profile* and your business *page* are not linked publicly, and no one can access your personal information from your business page. Now that you are all set up, let's go over some powerful Facebook strategies to get the most out of your Facebook page.

I am not going to review the steps needed to do something on your Facebook page since Facebook changes things so often that if I were to point out details about how to post a video or how to do something on your page, it would be outdated by the time you read it.

With Facebook, it's all about *strategy*. Strategies are as evergreen as you can get. Effective marketing strategies will serve you much longer than technical instructions on how to do something. I do realize that to implement some of the strategies here, you will need the technical know-how of the mechanics of doing that particular task and, for this, I will give you some great resources. Also remember that the *help* tab in Facebook is really useful for any information or definitions you need. For example, you can learn how to delete something on your page, learn more about a concept, or even learn how to post a video.

15 SUREFIRE FACEBOOK STRATEGIES FOR YOUR DENTAL PRACTICE

1. Optimize your Facebook page. It's so important to fill out all of your practice information, business hours, and descriptions about your office. The more information you have about your office, the more chances you'll have of your page being found.

2. Post pictures on your Facebook page. Post pictures of you and any other dentist that might be working with you. Make sure to post pictures of your team as patients want to see who else will be seeing them in the office. What types of pictures should you post? A good rule of thumb here is to post about 80 percent professional content and 20 percent personal. Remember that this is your business page, and you should be giving your patients or prospective patients useful and interesting content.

3. Claim your vanity name. This one is important for marketing since your Facebook page (business page), like your website, is also a URL that you send to people. Go to www.facebook.com/username to claim your username. When you create your Facebook page, you should also create your username by checking its availability and then picking something that you can market in your promotions. You should give out your Facebook URL or business page name as you would your website address. For example, our office page address is http://www.facebook.com/socalsmiles. Make sure your URL is similar to your practice name or the name that you'll be promoting.

4. Display an inviting and unique Facebook Timeline picture. When people land on your Facebook page they instantly get a *"feel"* for your brand and office. Is it unique or generic? Is it YOU? Are you displaying the best feel of your office? I know that a lot of this is subjective, but your Facebook Timeline picture should represent your brand, what your office feels like when they walk in, an overall uniqueness about you and your practice. For example, currently on our front page when people come to our Facebook address we have a picture of our front office. We take pride in the way our practice looks and feels so we wanted to display that image and feel to the online community. Let's keep this one simple and aim for something distinctively YOU!

5. Always post awesome content. No *strategy* takes the place of well-crafted, meaningful posts on your page. Post something that really adds value. Don't post about how you are hiring a new assistant. No one really cares. Add content like this every now and then, especially if you need a new assistant, but people don't want to see what your company needs on their news feed. What they do want is something interesting, creative, refreshing, and worthy of talking about. Rarely talk about promotions and offers on teeth whitening or Invisalign. Instead, always be the go-to *source for insight and education* on these topics.

Good content to post:

- Top foods for your teeth
- Healthy vitamins for your teeth and gums
- Five over-the-counter dental products you should be using
- The best all natural dental products
- Everything you need to know about Zoom teeth whitening
- Everything you need to know about Invisalign
- The best thing about cosmetic dentistry
- Causes of bad breath
- How to overcome bad breath
- The dangers of amalgam fillings

Also, be different! Here are some topics most dentists are afraid to talk about. But if you position yourself as the expert for your patients, they will always be yours.

- The hidden secrets of cosmetic dentistry
- The one thing dentists don't tell you about teeth whitening
- The 10 things you must know before going to the dentist

Recognize the value of these topics to the consumer. They have nothing to do with you promoting your office, but everything to do with educating your patients on topics they want to know more about. When you give out creative and informative content, you are also positioning yourself as the expert in your area. If you do this, your patients will see you as the *expert in your industry* and will *want* to come into your office and *buy* from you. They'll also ask for your opinion(your treatment plan) in regards to their dental condition.

6. Make a video and upload it onto Facebook. The topics above are great video ideas! You should be making short videos on each of these topics and placing them on your office's Facebook page. When you upload a video *directly* to Facebook, and someone(non-fan) sees your video, it will have a *like* button in the upper left-hand corner of the video. The advantage is that when someone watches and likes your video, they will automatically become a fan without going to your page. On the other hand, if you upload your video onto YouTube and then link it to your Facebook page, the viewer will not have the option to like it. The take-away point here is, if you are trying to increase your fan-base on Facebook, upload the video directly onto your Facebook page so people have the option to like your page via clicking *like* on the video.

7. Pull your blog into your Facebook page. All the above topics that I mentioned can also be made into articles and be posted on your blog. I will talk about your blog later, but just know that it is always best to send patients to read articles you posted on your blog rather than giving them a link that goes outside your footprint to someone else's blog or site. Got it? Keep them in your loop of influence and keep them in your social media footprint. To clarify, you might write something on your wall that says, "Want to know how to cure bad breath?" Check out my new article! And provide the link to your blog that would be located on your website.

Facebook also has an application called Networked Blogs. This is a really effective way to pull your blog into your Facebook page. Follow the instructions to set it up by going to http://apps.facebook.com/blognetworks/index.php. The instructions will walk you through the installation of your blog on your business page. The great thing about this is that everyone who visits your Facebook page can still stay on it while roaming around your blog that's within your page. If you do not install this application you can still send them to your blog by posting a link to it on your wall. They would leave Facebook and go straight to your blog. So, use Facebook to send people to your blog where you have even more interesting and in-depth content. You can either send them to your website, or by using Networked Blogs, you can direct them to another section of your Facebook page and still keep them on Facebook. Remember that everything in your social media footprint doesn't always have to be different. It's okay to post the same article on your blog, have a video on your YouTube, and a link to it on your Facebook page. The ultimate goal is to encourage interactivity, and you will soon see yourself having a greater influence across your diverse social media platforms.

8. Post a question to start a conversation. When you are watching a TV show or even listening to the news or radio don't they always find ways for you to return after a commercial break? Usually, they will say something like, "Coming up, the number one reason you, too, should eat dog food!" Even though you won't be eating dog food, you are tempted to come back or at least wait and see what they have to say out of curiosity. Curiosity keeps them coming back! I want you to keep this mind while posting your content on Facebook. Think of your posts in terms of *headlines*. If you post with an interesting question, you are likely to initiate some good conversation from your readers. Don't post "Brush more to prevent gingivitis." Instead post "What *do you think* are the top three things that prevent gum disease?" Another post might ask, "How many people find brushing their teeth painful?" or "Can you cure heart disease by brushing?" These are all conversation starters; they incite an internal dialogue, which prompts people to respond to your posts.

9. Use first names when replying to a post. This is a simple but powerful action. The sound that commands the most attention from people is their own name. This is especially true in conversations, but it also applies when connecting with your fans, patients, and visitors online. In general, people really like being called by their name. If you don't believe me, try it when you are out in a social setting and use the person's name. You'll find that they listen to what you are saying and that they better follow your path of conversation. The same rule applies on Facebook. Remember social media is word of mouth on Steroids! So, if you repeat online what you would do when you are talking to someone in-person, you will establish a deeper connection. Keep it cool, and when responding to a post or replying to a comment, use the person's name when you address them. In doing so, keep in mind that everyone else on that page will see what you wrote and to whom you wrote it.

10. **Talk about them.** Once again, in social settings, don't people love to talk about themselves? Of course they do. So, the same would apply on Facebook. Keep your posts or wall conversations about your fans or the person you are conversing with at the time. Don't always talk about your office or how cool teeth whitening can be or your new something that you just got. Talk about what's on *their* mind and remember to keep it professional since this is your business page. It's okay to throw in some interesting posts that you know will spark conversation, but if those posts can be about dentistry or even health, then you are in line with establishing yourself as the go-to expert. Remember, everything you do should be thought of as a strategy for adding value or creating *community value* that spurs interactivity and conversation. For example, the topic of your post could be how gum disease has been linked to heart disease or how moving teeth too fast while in braces can cause root resorption, while asking if anyone knew those things. Interesting facts with questions that spur interactivity are usually great. In your replies you can say that one of the differences between Invisalign and braces is the manner in which they move your teeth; one translates and the other one tips and torques. Now you can see how basic questions can turn into valuable insights for your potential patients and those already in your practice.

11. **Identify your page administrators.** Nobody likes (or wants) to talk to a brand. People like talking to people, so make sure your visitors know who is responding to them. If you are the only dentist in your office and your

picture is displayed, it's assumed that you are the one responding. My recommendation is to have a few of your trusted team members, such as your office manager or an associate doctor, assigned as page administrators. This way, a few people can respond to questions or comments. Even so, make sure they sign off using their professional name. It may look something like this: "Hey John, thanks for the input. We loved seeing you the other day."-- Dr. Brown. When you sign your name to a post, your fans know who posted that response. Another more organized way to identify your page administrators is by having a section on your page dedicated to them. It's like a meet-your-dentist section, which shares with your fans a little information about who is talking to them and posting content for them on a regular basis. Let me emphasize that even though you have administrators who can respond to comments and post content on your page, you really should spend five to ten minutes a day interacting with people and posting your own content. It's nice to see the dentist interacting with patients online; this is important, and you should think of it as talking to your patients, even though they're not in your chair just yet. Make it a consistent priority, and you'll see it doesn't take too long to do if you do it daily.

12. Optimize your e-mail signature. Everyone uses e-mail, yet most people just sign off with their name. An official e-mail signature can be an automatic and easy way to build your Facebook community. Every time you send an e-mail, the recipient will see the link to your Facebook page and can easily click on it. It's easy, and it's automatic, and you should put this one into effect immediately. If you use a web-based e-mail service, check out this great tool for adding e-mail signatures: http://www.WiseStamp. com

13. PlugIN to your website. This one is a *must* for everyone who has a website. Facebook can easily be plugged into your website. This simply means that on your website, you can have a small summary box of your fans and a *like* button so that people coming to your website can see a snapshot of your Facebook page. You can easily have your webmaster install this on your website by having them go to http://developers.facebook. com/docs/guides/web/. This is a section with instruction for integrating

Facebook features right into your site. You can go to my site at http://www.socalsmiles.net to see how a Facebook plug-in currently looks. Note: The appearance of these plug-ins can change at any time. By the time you read this book, many other forms and types of similar plug-ins will be available. The main point here is to bring them to your site to keep your message and brand connected across all elements of your Online Presence Triangle.

14. Create a posting plan. When are you going to post your content? Don't take the weekends off because many people read posts during their time off work, which means they're accessing their Facebook accounts on the weekend. Research has shown us that people are more responsive and check their Facebook accounts in the morning, then on weekends, and then on certain days like Tuesday and Sunday. Don't get too focused on these statistics because they will likely change as social media and its integration into our lifestyle evolves.

How often do you and your fans interact with each other? The affinity score goes up the more you interact with people. In other words, the more you interact with fans on your site, the better your future posts will be received in their newsfeeds. For instance, if you never interacted with someone and then randomly decided to post something, it might not appear on his or her newsfeed. If your interactions were more consistent, however, your posts are more likely to show on their newsfeed. This is part of Facebook's interactivity algorithm. A great way to strengthen this is by always responding to those who comment on your page. Keep the conversation going and respond back; this way, your fans will know that it's an active page and will more likely respond the next time you post.

15. Create fan-only content. Think of unique content that you can display for your new fans. As soon as they click the *like* button, they should be directed to a page or video just for fans. This can even be the gift you are giving away to new fans who have signed up. Or, maybe it's a video or an e-book. Regardless, interact with them; show them that your page is *alive* and not just another page. I think you get the point here.

QUICK TIPS ON GETTING MORE FANS AND PATIENTS

Send a page suggestion to your patients. This is a quick way for you to boost your "Likes" on your Facebook page and build your community. Extract all of the e-mails from your practice software system and put them onto a spreadsheet. Then, go to your Facebook page, click on *edit page,* and select *resources* in the right-hand pane. Once you are on this new page select *Tell your Fans* and upload all of your patients' e-mail addresses. Facebook will then send an e-mail to all of your patients to suggest that they *like* your page. Stay engaged! Having your existing patients come to your Facebook page will make it possible for you to interact with them regularly.

Suggest a page like on your appointment page. Get more fans as you get more online appointments. Everyone who makes an online appointment has to go to your appointment page on your website. Right before they press *submit* and enter their information to make that appointment request, you can place an alert that explains if they "Like" you on Facebook, they receive 5 percent off any dental treatment for the online appointment that was made. So, if the appointment was for a crown you can deduct 5 percent when they make that appointment. Do you see how this strategy connects your website to your Facebook page? Use this technique to acquire more "likes" as you get more online appointments. I still use this little trick and it works great!

Facebook advertising. Facebook Ads are awesome! It's a reminder of the power and effect customized and targeted marketing can have on your practice. If you go to your Facebook page and click on *edit page*, you can access the controllable parameters for your page. From here, select *marketing* and then *Advertise on Facebook.* In five minutes you can create a mini-ad that is seen on the side of people's profiles and pages. The best part? Your ad reaches a specific audience. You can target them based on age, sex, where they live, where they work, and even their interests. Once you refine your target audience, Facebook will also tell you the *estimate reach* for that audience, which is the number of people within Facebook that are in your search criteria who would see your ad. What would this mean for your practice? Well, look up the ten largest local businesses around you, and target those people. Even better, find out which businesses have the best insurances that are great for your office and target those businesses. You can easily find out what type of insurance Verizon has in your area by calling their human resources department. Think of it this way: your services could possibly reach people who may be currently looking for them. How about fashion models? Don't you think they would want whiter, straighter, better-looking teeth? You could target local modeling agencies and promote a teeth whitening offer. The list of prospective patients goes on and on.

After creating an ad and learning about who you want to target, you must choose where you want them to land after they click on your ad. A great place is your appointments page on your website. For instance, if you create an ad about teeth whitening, have them land on a page in your website that explains teeth whitening with an area right there where they can make an appointment. What would you want to have on this page on your website? How about some video testimonials from actual patients that you have seen?

Facebook Groups. Facebook Groups allows you to integrate your expertise as a dentist to any other group currently out there. You might find a group on health and nutrition, beauty, body care, or the countless other groups that are active on Facebook. Join some of these groups and become known as the expert dentist in your area. You can then start commenting on the different topics and posts in the group and integrate your expertise this way as well.

INTEGRATING YOUTUBE WITH FACEBOOK

You can even pull all of your YouTube videos onto your Facebook page, which helps to keep all areas of your content connected. When people see your Facebook page, they can also see all of your YouTube videos. Check out www.involver.com to customize your Facebook experience with many other components, such as coupons, contests, landing pages, and other resources outside of Facebook. Great for integration!

We have gone through a lot of tactical information on how to use Facebook to keep adding consistent value to your patients and those who search for your services. Remember that Facebook is just one tool to help you maximize the impact on your patients' lives. Seven years ago it didn't even exist, and seven years from now, who knows where it will be.

One thing will stay the same. Relating to people via social media tactics and strategies will grow and improve, so if the tool changes you will still have the methods, strategies, and the skills that you have learned to communicate with your patients and community. The information, mindset, strategies, and keys to online patient interaction is more important than any tool that we have reviewed in this book. You now have the ability to spread your services, thoughts, and ideas to a widespread audience that wants to know more about what you have to offer.

Chapter 21

YOUTUBE- YOUR OWN TV CHANNEL

Lights, camera, action!

Talking about YouTube is a topic that I love! Before we hit the big screen with this online video giant, I want you to remember exactly what YouTube was, still is, and will be. YouTube is *user-generated* content. *User-generated* means ordinary people like you and I are posting content or videos that are practically homemade without the use of expensive equipment and producers. These videos are made with the ordinary tools that we as dentists have access to, and it's these types of videos that get the most views and are high in demand. So, every time doctors tell me that they don't want to be bothered with assembling all this, I tell them all they really need are a few simple things.

All you have to do is make raw, authentic, visually functional videos and upload them onto YouTube. By now, the idea of videos should really be engraved into your mind considering everything we have already reviewed. As a dentist, YouTube is the best place to upload your video content and, in this chapter, you will learn how to open and populate your own TV channel via YouTube. But first, a few YouTube facts:

YouTube

- Has 4 billion videos viewed per day.
- Has 600 million mobile views a day and growing rapidly!
- Has 60 hours of video uploaded on their site every single minute.
- Has 3 billion videos that make money every week.
- Has 70 percent of its videos being viewed outside of the United States. Now your office can go global! Remember that you may be creating content for people who live outside the United States.
- Is now owned by Google. Google is now directing their users' search results to YouTube webpages and its video site.
- Has a homepage that is dynamic and social.
- Has a homepage that has been sold out for over a year. That's right. The front page on YouTube has been sold out for over a year in advance.

Wow! I feel a surge of business potential every time I read through these YouTube facts. To really understand how we can benefit from YouTube, we must first understand how videos can impact our practices. The concept of video is mentioned throughout this entire book. Video gives us the ability to *show* our story to our audience. I said *show* not *tell*! It enables us to give our audience (our prospective patients) a glimpse inside our world before committing. Your patients can get to know you, feel comfortable with you, and learn from you before spending their money. Give first, and then receive. Video enables you to give to your patients before they ever have to purchase anything from you. I hope that I have made my case very clear about the power of video content. Remember these facts about videos, and you will never underestimate the message that your office can spread via two minutes with a handheld camera.

We have already reviewed some great video content ideas. Earlier we said that your video content can be split up into five main categories. We have already outlined these categories, but I want to discuss how to use them with YouTube. Doctors always ask me, "Well, I got some patients on video talking about their great experience at the office, but what do I do with it now? Do I just place it on my website or something?" The clear answer here is a *partial* no. Randomly uploading videos on your site doesn't lead people back to your office. In order to create a social media footprint here, your content should link your other content together so that it tells a story or creates your brand. You want everything to come together to form a nice melody—not some random noise with scattered content. Keep this in mind.

Now that you have your video, what do you do with it? Where do you place it, and who do you show and tell? First, if you haven't done so already, go to YouTube.com and sign up your office for its own YouTube channel. This is really like having your own TV channel. It's free and takes five minutes. If your office is named after you, use that as the channel name. But if it's something else like *South County Smiles,* use that since that is what you are and will be branding. Let me give you a word of advice here if your office name is the same as your name. If you practice in Houston, Texas, and your name is Dr. John Smith, I would not call your YouTube channel *drjohnsmith* because no one really knows who that is. Call it instead *HoustonDentistTV* (Be sure to stay within the character limit) or even *HoustonDentist.* This way, your TV channel will be instantly recognizable when you send a channel invite. Another thing it will do is optimize any videos you create for your office since anyone that searches for *Houston Teeth Whitening* will be more likely to come across *HoustonDentist.*

YouTube has variety of templates from which to choose when designing your homepage, but my recommendation is to get a web designer either online or through a referral source. Your YouTube page design should match your website or the brand that you want to market to your prospective patients. Don't get stuck on this part since there are millions of resources that you can use to accomplish this, some of which have been listed here as web resources. Now that you have your channel, you have a place to put your content. Take your videos, upload them onto your Mac or PC and instantly send or share them.

But how will you identify your videos? Use these three points to identify your video with. First, give your video a *title.* Second, give your video a *description* and, third, give it some *tags.* Let's quickly go over these.

Video title: This should be the title of your video based on searches for keywords. For example, if you shot a video about teeth whitening, make your title something like *Teeth Whitening in Costa Mesa* or *Teeth Whitening Dentist in Orange County*. Don't use titles such as *cool whitening* or *whiter teeth in an hour* or *get white teeth with Zoom*. These phrases are too generic and focus on the procedure too much. Your focus should instead be on the procedure and how it relates to you and your office. A good idea is to put your city or region into your video title. Remember, most people searching for a dentist are not going to search *Dentist in California*; instead, they will search for specific local regions. This is called a local search, and dentistry is a local-search business for the most part. For instance, if you shoot a video on how cavities are formed, the title can be *Houston dentist talks about cavities* or *Newport Beach dentist discusses cavities*. Now, when someone searches for dentists in Houston, your video will more than likely get indexed by Google because you have a title that matches their search parameters. Don't get me wrong. Google and most other search engines regularly change their search algorithm *but common sense and consistency with matching phrases and similar terminology across your related content will always give any algorithm a clear message as to where that content originated.*

Video description: Once you pick a title with some strong keywords, you must give your video a short description. Always begin your description with your URL, including the http://. For example, if your website is www.socalsmiles.net, make sure you add the http:// in front to make it http://www.socalsmiles.net. This will make it a clickable link in your description. In short, this is one more way people can click on your link and go to your website. Here is an example of a full description:

http://www.socalsmiles.net Dr. Ganatra is a teeth whitening dentist in Costa Mesa. In this video, he shows you how white your teeth can get at his dental office in Costa Mesa. To see more, check out his website or call 800-123-4567. Do you see how this is leading them back to your office?

Video tags: After you write up the description, add some tags. Tags are simply the keywords that identify your video when people search for similar content. For the whitening video, the tags might be *teeth whitening, dentist, Costa Mesa, Zoom whitening,* or *cosmetic dentistry*—all related to getting your teeth whitened. Also, be sure to put the keywords associated with your local search area, such as the region or city. Make sure you cover some of the most obvious keywords as well as the ones that are related. Now, you are ready to upload your video.

Now that your video is on YouTube, we need to get some people looking it at. It's time to get some eyeballs on your video so that you can start publicizing your office, your content, and business. **Ask your webmaster to place the YouTube videos on your website.** This is why I said taking your video and uploading it immediately was a *partial* no. You should *first* upload it onto YouTube, and then your website. You see, YouTube is one of many video players that you can use to place videos on your site. If you go to www.socalsmiles.net, you can see how our YouTube videos are embedded on our site. Do you see how it all connects? **Your YouTube channel holds all of the video content *and then* from there, you place some of that content on your site.** This gives your videos more views as well.

Here is another tip for getting more views: **Use the autoplay feature.** Ask your webmaster to set the videos on autoplay when they're uploaded to the website. When people visit your homepage, your video automatically starts playing. The autoplay feature is easily activated on the *videos & playlists* tab on your YouTube homepage. On your website, your webmaster inputs some web code (html) to activate it. By doing this, alone, your videos will have more views. Once again, do you see how the triangle is connecting all the elements? Once your YouTube video is embedded onto your website or blog, you can even e-mail your patients inviting them to check out your new video.

As you start placing more useful content on your YouTube channel, you will want subscribers. This is yet another way to spread the word about your brand and office. I want to address a concern you might have. Adding friends and subscribers to your YouTube channel won't suddenly result in a ton of new, local patients. On the other hand, you will be using YouTube to host most of your videos. Be okay with the fact that you are not targeting everyone near your office using your YouTube channel, at least not yet. This type of specificity is not available through YouTube. Remember that the world is a small place today, and it's getting even smaller. Don't think that since you live and practice in Los Angeles you would only want people that live in Los Angeles watching your videos. This is far from the truth since as a dentist and business, brand exposure to as many people as possible is valuable. Everything is connected online so that if people in New York know about you and you are creating great content, they may know of someone near your area that needs your services. Maybe a dental supply vendor watches your videos and wants you to promote their product as well. Don't think small and feel that you have to be marketing only to patients nearby.

In addition, you don't know of the other opportunities and increased patient awareness that may result. As dentists, we are all small business owners, but haven't you had people visit your office who have heard about you from others that don't even live nearby? I certainly have. Don't let your small business make you small-minded. So, how do you create a strong following on YouTube?

Your tribe of followers on YouTube is your subscribers and friends. Here is the psychology behind building this tribe effectively. Your YouTube channel is a dental office channel that plays content related to dental health, teeth, nutrition, and even lifestyle related to well-being. Don't look at your video voice outlet as just dentistry and teeth because, in actuality, you and your office are beyond that.

GETTING FRIENDS AND SUBSCRIBERS: THE STRATEGY

Believe it or not, millions of people would love to know about the content in your videos. But where are these people, and who are they? To find people interested in the content you are creating, simply search for them on YouTube. As a dentist you would type *Costa Mesa dentist, Zoom teeth whitening in California, porcelain veneers, root canals,* or even *healthy living.* Other videos related to these keywords will pop up. Click on one of the channels and see how many subscribers there are. Then, send out friend requests to all of those channels' subscribers. Why? If those people are subscribing to content similar to what your channel is creating, it's likely they will subscribe or *friend you* on your channel as well. You can go to every single subscriber or friend already on other people's channels and send them a message or request that they subscribe to your channel. Let's say you search for a dentist in your area and you find that 200 people subscribe to their channel. Since you share similar interests, all you would do is send each of them a request to subscribe to your channel.

I know you are probably thinking that you have no time to do all of this YouTube stuff! What if I told you that growing your YouTube presence can be automatic and can happen while you sleep? Let me share an amazing tool with you! It's called *Tube Toolbox,* and it automates everything that I just reviewed. Go to *www.TubeToolBox.com* for more information. Why wouldn't you build more of a brand when you know about others in your niche? Why wouldn't you want them to watch your videos? Tube Toolbox can run while you sleep and can have you pick up more friends and subscribers in just a few days. Remember the more your content is strategically distributed via your social media footprint, the more presence your office has across the Web. This is just one way to build that presence with people all around the world.

You could also invite(via email) your patients who already have a YouTube channel to your channel so that they can subscribe to your videos and promote your office to their own friends and family. **This is a situation where locality and an actual patient-base will benefit your office via a strong YouTube presence.** Also, let's not forget that Google owns YouTube and the more quality content with well-crafted titles, keywords, and tags you have in your YouTube videos, the better your overall presence will be during related search results.

Here are 5 strategies to optimize the impact of your videos:

1. Music is a great attention grabber, and putting some fun and interesting music in any part of your video can really boost views as people like good music combined with creative video.
2. Placing your website address and phone number on the lower third of your video is a great way to keep your audience informed. You should have this showing for the entire video.
3. Always end the video with your information and phone number at the end of the video as well. You can write, *"Appointments available at phone*

number and website." This is a non-direct way of telling your viewers that appointments are available.

4. Call to action. Always tell people to comment on what they thought of your video at the end of your video.

5. *Don't* always tell them to make an appointment. This may come as a surprise to you. Remember, you want your audience to know you are making these videos to create and relate to them via your important value-added material. If you are always asking them to make an appointment, people will eventually get the idea that you are out there just to get them in the office. Be genuine and sincere about your content creation and viewer relations.

YouTube provides a world of opportunities and exposure. It enables you to host your own TV channel and to send your message of dentistry and wellness to the world. Start creating some great content through what you have learned here, and put it up on YouTube. YouTube is getting even bigger and more powerful, and videos are driving the content revolution in dentistry and the world. See you there!

Chapter 22

YOUR BLOG

*A journal of thoughts, ideas, and insights illuminates
your message to your patients.*

Your blog is a big part of your Social Media Footprint. Think of your blog as a place for your ideas, thoughts, concepts, and the messages you want to impart. For example, you may have a video explaining to your patients how gum disease increases the likelihood of heart disease. Your patients might love watching you talk about this, but what if they also read something about it on your blog. Maybe you could have a video about some topic on your blog and under the video you could write about the same topic as well. Would that present the information to them from a different prospective? *You see, your message must get to your patients before they get to you.* Now, you're probably thinking, *Who the heck has time to write an article after posting a video?* It really doesn't take long to draft an article on a familiar topic in dentistry. Put out a few bulleted points and information you want to review with your patients, and write out some details about those points. Another alternative is to hire someone for around $5–$10 per hour and have them research and write an article about your topic. I've done this many times when I simply didn't have the time between patients, charts, and my personal life.

The following websites are excellent, inexpensive resources for getting articles and written content populated on your blog. In addition, you will find that they have a multitude of other things that can be done for a very competitive price. oDesk.com and Elance.com are both favorites of mine for outsourcing these types of tasks. For the sake of quality articles for your blog, let's talk about these two amazing resources. There are thousands of people waiting to work for you, to write that article or blog for a reasonable price. What's great about these two sites is that the virtual contractors' work history is transparent with reviews and feedback from previous employers. For example, you can see the last job that they completed and what rating they earned from the person who hired them. You can read the comments that were written about their work, the timeliness of meeting deadlines, and their effectiveness in communications. These are just a few of the attributes you can evaluate before you decide to hire. You can also see what type of tests they've taken that may relate to the skill set you require. Visit oDesk.com or Elance.com and see for yourself. With the advent of these types of sites, you have no excuse *not* to write an article.

Now that we've thrown some outsourcing power into the mix, what else can your blog do for you? When you have a blog, you should also have a *comments box* underneath your content. **Make sure you place the Facebook comments plug-in for your comments section.** What does that mean? You see the style of those Facebook comments on your Facebook page? You can replicate that on your blog! So, when someone comments on your blog, it can also post to that person's Facebook page for everyone on their page to see. You can easily tell your webmaster to integrate this into your blog. Others see their friends commenting on your blog, so they go to your blog to check out the hype: your article, video, or any other content you've posted. This gives your blog some traffic and also makes it more likely they'll click on the appointment link to make an appointment. This is one way of making the content you post gain mass exposure.

BLOG LAYOUT

A blog is more about interacting with your patient-base and prospective patients than your website is. I say this because all a blog really does is push your valuable content out to your viewers. The people who follow your blog will come back for more. If they are your patients, then you are staying at *top of mind* with them. If they are not yet your patients, then you are marketing or consistently adding massive value! Either way you look at it, your blog can highly influence the *attraction* stage and the *return* stage with your patients. Make it easy for them to come into your office from your blog alone. Have an appointment button in your blog for online appointments. Once they click on *make an appointment*, they can be directed to your appointment page on your website and whamo you got an appointment! What else should you have on your blog?

Once you send patients to your blog, they'll receive some amazing value-added content from you. This can be in the form of a video, articles, interesting tidbits on health, and so on. The main point is to establish yourself as the *expert* in your community. Let's say you post something really interesting on your blog every month. Your patients will send this information to their friends, and they, too, will read or watch what you posted. You are now exposing yourself, your practice, and vision to other prospective patients who may want your services, simply because they liked what you posted on your blog.

Just like the YouTube videos, make sure you use the appropriate tags and keywords to identify your blog post. If you are a dentist in Newport Beach, the title of your blog article might be, "Newport Beach dentist talks about bad breath." Then, make your tags, titles, and keywords relate to your locality so that you are search engine friendly. Your tags could be *Newport Beach, dentist, bad breath, dental health,* or *dental cleaning.* Keep all of your words relevant to your content.

5 KEY ELEMENTS TO A WINNING DENTAL BLOG

1. **Keep it personal:** Blogs are more personal than websites. People read blogs because they want to hear about you and learn from you. They want to know what you have to offer. They look for pictures of you, your office, and your team. Pictures let your readers know that someone is actually writing and responding on that blog. If you have multiple doctors in your office, have a picture of each who respond and post content. Patients want to engage with you on your blog, so create an engaging environment there.

2. **Keep it interactive**: Interaction is a two-way street. One of the most important things, we said earlier, was that your website should immediately give something away to the visitor. The same applies to your blog, but remember that your blog simply holds content, which means it's already giving something away. It's giving information. So, how do you capture names and e-mails? The best way is to give them a free video series, a report, or something of value in exchange for their information. You may even want to give away a special dental service, such as teeth whitening or a limited-time deal on Invisalign. For example, if you post an article about Invisalign or teeth whitening, promote one or the other with specials for a month or so. When people come to your blog, they expect to learn something more about your topic or service, and that's the purpose of your blog.

By blogging, you are drawing in a very specific audience; so, in this case, it's okay to give them a free whitening or a deal on Invisalign, or even a special promotion just for visiting your blog. *Your blog will have a loyal following from your really interested fan-base because it holds specific content your viewers look for.* Your website holds some of that, but it also reveals all the broad spectrum of services your business offers. Your blog, on the other hand, truly gives people the content they are searching for and answers to specific questions. Your blog is a great place to start building that *tribe of followers* that really wants to hear from you.

3. **Keep it looking like your website:** This is important because you want the look of your website and office to be reflected in your blog. You don't

want your blog to look totally different than your website. You should have one web designer for both and integrate them appropriately.

4. Keep it fresh: No one likes to eat cookies out of a nearly empty bowl. Re-fill your bowl! Don't restaurants keep food on the buffet tables fresh and re-filled? You should aim to do the same with your blog content. If you haven't posted anything in months or years, they will assume you have nothing new to contribute. You can't expect people to come back to something that never gets refreshed with new content. You should update your blog weekly. This shows that someone is home and active.

5. Keep it connected: Your blog should also connect to your Facebook page and back to your website as well. You can have your webmaster install a Facebook section on your blog that shows all of your recent status updates and friends. This lets people know you are connected on Facebook.

THE ONLINE PRESENCE TRIANGLE IN ACTION

So, how do we tie this all together? How does your blog relate to your e-mail, video, Facebook, and any other online resources? Let's say you post an interesting article on the top five foods that are great for your teeth and overall health. Here are the ways you can make the Triangle work for you:

Scenario #1
Post this on Facebook: *"Something so good for your health is also good for your teeth?"* Include with this post a link to your blog. This is done right. It poses a question, ignites curiosity, and attracts people with a desire to find out. They'll *want to click on it.* When they do click on it, it sends them to your blog where they can read more about your Facebook post.

Scenario #2

Send an e-mail to your patients with the following subject line: *"Health, Teeth, Good?" --Dr. Ganatra.* What is so right about this? It spurs curiosity, immediately tells them it's from their dentist, it's short and sweet, and it confirms that you are not trying to sell something since the subject line is an informative one. Patients open their e-mail and click on the link to check out your blog.

Scenario #3

Upload a video to Facebook and then grab the embed code to paste that same video on your blog. (Your webmaster can do this in a matter of minutes.) This video will now be viewed on Facebook's video player. For example, when you see a YouTube video, it has the YouTube logo in the lower right-hand corner of the video because that is the player in which you are viewing it. In this case, you will view your video on the Facebook player since you grabbed the embed code off of Facebook after uploading your video. The coolest thing about this player is that when your video plays on your blog and the person watching it has not *liked* your page, it will give them an option to do so as they are watching that video. Having this option on your video increases the number of people that will *like* your Facebook business page from your blog, which increases your fan-base on Facebook and builds your online community of patients.

Do you see how all of these scenarios hold the triangle together? How all those arrows literally direct you from one to the other? This is the secret to having success online. You are not only engaging with the maximum number of prospective patients and existing patients, but you are also building your presence. As you continue building it, you will see that *presence brings patients!*

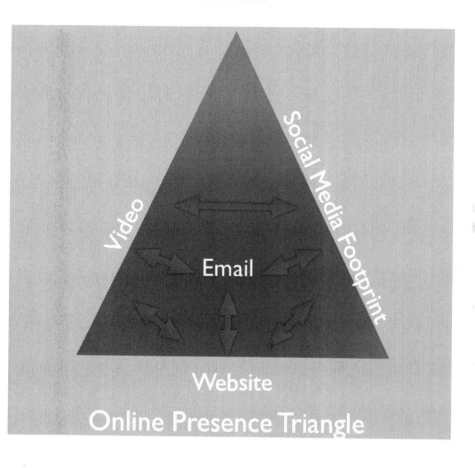

Chapter 23

TWITTER FOR DENTISTS

Small nuggets of information are starting to change the world.

Twitter has over 300 million subscribers. It's estimated that the number of Twitter followers increases by 300,000 every day. But what does it mean to you and growing you practice and engaging your patients? This chapter isn't going to give you a Twitter attack strategy to bring in large numbers of patients. But it will emphasize the reason that you and your practice should be communicating through Twitter.

Let me start off by saying that for dentists, I really don't think using Twitter is as effective as the other strategies that I have reviewed in this book. Using Facebook effectively, posting videos on YouTube, and adding valuable content on your blog is far more effective than tweeting 140-character nuggets of information. So if you have been doubtful that you can get loads of patients to your office and make a real impact with Twitter for your practice then I would agree, but I wouldn't totally ignore Twitter either.

Now that we know that search results on Google include relevant social media content, you also must be tweeting this content. The easiest way to do this is to connect your Twitter account to your Facebook account. This is a simple settings adjustment that you can make so that whenever you post something on your Facebook page, it will automatically be tweeted out through your Twitter profile.

Go to Twitter.com and enter your practice information, and create a Twitter profile. It's easy to do and takes less than ten minutes. For example, my office name is *SoCal Smiles Dentistry,* and my twitter address is @socalsmiles. Remember to keep it consistent so that you can be easily found and identified. If you are using your name as your dental practice name, keep that as your Twitter profile as well. If the office's name is *Costa Mesa Dentist,* then keep that as your Twitter name. Pick from one of the many professional background themes that Twitter offers, or hire a web designer to make a custom theme for you that incorporates elements from your website and office. The latter would be my suggestion, as you really should make your brand online as distinct and unique as possible.

The Twitter *advanced search* feature is a useful Twitter function. Basically, you can search for any keyword or phrase that has been tweeted or talked about in your area within a certain time frame. Really cool! But what does it mean? Well, if you live in Los Angeles, you can search for *wisdom tooth* and see who is talking about wisdom teeth or even getting them out. When you do find relevant search topics, you can then interact with those people and answer questions with your tweets. This may direct some of those people back to your office. Once again, I would not count on this as a means to get people into your office. But use it to start conversations and raise the level of awareness about your services and office location. Remember to post links to your blog or even video links back to your YouTube site on your Twitter page for everyone to see.

For you to have any sort of presence on Twitter, you should be tweeting on a regular basis, and it should be something related to dentistry. We have reviewed many topics for short videos. Those same topics can be tweets that send people to your blog or website. For instance you could tweet, *"I just posted a great video on Invisalign: www.yourwebsite.com."* If you just wrote a new blog post, tweet to your followers about this, and drive them to your blog.

THE BASICS OF BUILDING A TWITTER FOLLOWING

The most effective way to build a Twitter following is to interact with relevant people. Don't try to follow every random person out there and hope they follow you back. It's much more important to have *relevant* followers who are genuinely interested in what you have to say. Start off by first following other dentists in your area. Type the word *dentist* in the search box, and a bunch of dentists will pop up. Look at their profiles and follow all the ones who interest you. Remember, they are not competitors; look at them as peers. Also, search for terms that may be related to the type of people that may need your services. You can search local modeling agencies that may be interested in teeth whitening, or even local public health services, schools, and other organizations that may have large followings. Follow these people and organizations, and some of them may follow you back. When they do follow you back, you know that they are receiving your tweets and are interested in your content. Start with interesting dental-related tweets and links on your profile, and create value for your followers. Be sure you are also directing them to your website and blog through your relevant links. If you do this consistently, you'll begin to build a following on Twitter.

My goal for you in this chapter was not to turn you into a Twitter master. My goal was to provide an introduction and get you tweeting and interacting on Twitter. It will keep you connected to yet another important social media element. I do understand that if this becomes too time consuming, it will likely not be done. But at least link your Facebook page updates to your Twitter profile so that you can shoot out an automatic tweet every time you post relevant content on Facebook.

In summary, get on Twitter but focus most of your time on all the other elements we have reviewed in this book. I think Twitter is a powerhouse communicator, but for us dentists, using video, Facebook, and your blog are more effective if done using the strategies and intentions I have laid out in this book.

Chapter 24

RE-INVENTING
DENTISTRY

I wish you a practice that recreates itself regularly, and growth that re-invents your brand every day. Expand the boundaries of what is possible within your business, and then commit to turning those possibilities into creative and unique ways in which you serve your patients.

C ongratulations! I hope I have refreshed your perspective on dentistry and all that is possible in our exciting profession. I am ever growing and always committed to uncovering new and exciting ways to push my practices to another level beyond just production and collection reports. I hope that you, too, are committed to making your dream practice possible for yourself, your team, and your patients. Be easy on yourself; the toughest part about everything you have read is just getting started. After you get started and get the wheels in motion, things will begin to happen and you will claim your creativity.

We have covered a tremendous amount of material within the pages of this book. I urge you to keep this as a reference as you practice the strategies and techniques outlined. Knowledge is not power, but action is. You must utilize what you know and begin living it in your practice. Only then can you really experience and learn what we've reviewed. Knowing it cognitively is the very base level of learning something, but doing it physically and integrating it into your practice is the only way this book will ever benefit you. You can use all the perspectives you may have picked up from this book by incorporating that psychology into your monthly meetings. Talk to your team about ATR, and tell them to focus on connecting with patients, and integrate the treatment plan and marketing insights into your practice immediately.

In this final chapter, I want to give you a roadmap with a starting point for your new journey. Realize that only 15 percent of the people who buy books actually read beyond the first chapter! This is quite alarming when you think about it. You've come this far, and you're already ahead of the game!

Begin by creating your Online Presence Triangle. If you don't already have a website, then get one up as soon as possible! Use the chapter on websites as your guide. Then, go to Google and claim your Google Places page so that you can start expanding your presence online. As you get your site up and claim your Google Places page, create some quick, informative videos for your patients and those visiting your site. Once you have your office name, your website, and have officially claimed your listing on Google, it's time to get on Facebook and YouTube. Start here before you post anything on your blog. Create your Facebook business page, and start spreading the word that your office is on Facebook and you've added some cool content and videos for patients to see. You can even send your whole patient database an e-mail suggesting they become a fan and *like* your page. Interact with your community, and have fun doing so. Get some patient testimonials as they come in for treatment, and encourage them to refer their friends and family to you as well. I know you are going to create some raving fans, so have them bring you even more patients by asking them to do so!

After you begin to establish yourself online, get connected to your team and use their talents to build your brand and business within the community. Start training your team for success. Engrave the mind-set of the ATR framework within your office. Have them see the value in not only bringing in new patients but also getting patients to come back for more treatment while referring others to do the same.

Dentistry is a challenging, yet very professionally and personally rewarding profession. You now have the ability to make a massive impact on the lives of your patients outside of your office as well. Utilize what you've learned here and continue learning from the best. Nothing that you have read here will matter unless you put it into action. In order for you to be successful, keep these three important elements in mind:

1. **Practice a championship mind-set:** Success is all about creating the most empowering mind-set for yourself and realizing that anything is possible as long as you *first believe it to be*. This is where most people fail before they have a chance to start; they come up with some excuse or negative thinking pattern before they even begin the journey. You might try to convince yourself of all the reasons you can't do something, but my advice to you is to resist falling for this disempowering reality. One of my mentors, Tony Robbins, taught me to tell myself, "If you can't, you must." Keep this in mind as you stretch beyond your boundaries and realize that anything worth achieving, creating, or becoming resides outside of your comfort zone. Make sure your mind-set empowers you to live outside of your comfort zone because that is where true success lies. So, go and get *Uncomfortable!*

2. **Take action *now*:** When you first read something, begin to learn something, or even start something new, you will not automatically be great at it! But don't let that keep you from immediate action. *Successful people take imperfect action and correct it along the way, while unsuccessful people are always trying to perfect the plan and never get started.* Be the few that do versus the many that just talk about it. After reading each chapter, write down some action items that you can follow up on, and get started today! There may be a phone call you need to make, or someone that you need to email, get the ball rolling! Otherwise nothing that we have reviewed here will create a change in your business or your life.

3. **Keep learning and creating:** Be an incessant learner and make sure you never get to a point where you feel like you know everything. Attend seminars, take CE courses, and think of *creative ways to be creative.*

Ask yourself the questions that will create more value for your patients and your practice. What more can I do for those who refer to me? How else can a patient's first visit be the start of a long-term relationship with our office? What's one positive quality about my team that I can help them expand upon even more? Ask the right questions that will empower your entire team to think deeper about your marketing campaigns. Remember, if marketing is consistently adding massive value, how else can you and your team do that? Even one small idea can create a colossal effect on your practice.

If you focus on these three areas, you will be able to create a practice that soars beyond your expectations. You don't have to be able to do everything I reviewed here, but look at what you need out of what we've covered, and integrate it into your unique style. Create beyond what is already created, and expect more from yourself and your practice than what your patients will ever expect of you. If you do this, you will have successfully Re-Invented Dentistry for Yourself.

APPENDIX

This is another exciting section of the book. It is specifically meant for those of you who want to jumpstart the knowledge you've acquired from particularly useful sections of the book and integrate it with other marketing and practice growth resources out there. I suggest you all do this. I have condensed some creative thoughts and ideas here for you to utilize in your practice as I have used many of these in my offices with great success. Some of the content is included from meetings that I have had with my own staff. The Groupon section reviews the setup and preparation your office must know about to successfully run a Groupon or any other type of social marketing promotion. The section on Daily Performance Goals was taken directly from my office meeting in which we implemented some powerful strategies for getting patients back into the office using a collective approach. The section on Demandforce is especially beneficial since it can really amplify what you've already learned here. I use it in my offices and wouldn't practice without it! Many years of learning, failure, and learning again have contributed to the insights achieved in this section alone. Enjoy!

SOCIAL MARKETING: FROM COUPONS TO GROUPON!

The first month I opened my office in Costa Mesa, California, I got sixty new patients, spent around $5,000, and got some traffic into the office. I did this using print marketing based on the type of services my patients wanted. Not bad, right? The first month, we collected around $45,000. All of this was done using the same principles we talked about in this book. Yes, it definitely paid the rent and kept the business and team going strong. But there's a problem here. *Our presence* was only as good as the graphics on that print ad, which is why print marketing and advertising is losing its impact. Your practice and your presence are bigger than what you can fit on a piece of paper.

I would be overseeing a marketing powerhouse if I didn't discuss the emergence and technique of social or collective buying. *I received 227 new patients within twenty-four hours* with no cost to me, aside from supply and the already present business setup of staff and location. **No other technique in all of my marketing experience has gotten me this many patients, this fast, while increasing exposure about our office brand and presence.**

Social or collective buying has skyrocketed since 2009! This is how it works: you and hundreds of thousands of other subscribers get an e-mail with a daily or short-term deal on a service your practice offers. You click on the deal in your e-mail to see how many other people have purchased that same deal and how long the deal will be offered. Groupon.com was one of the first platforms to really initiate the power of collective buying via an online e-mail platform. Here are four of the greatest reasons for this type of platform when marketing your office:

1. Your entire web presence is exposed to thousands of potential patients. Even if they don't actually purchase the deal that day, they still see your office name as it quickly spreads online. As a business, this is a tremendous leverage point since the majority of buying decisions

today are influenced by some sort of online research before a purchase it ever made.

2. If your online presence is set up correctly (using the Online Presence Triangle, for example), you can actually capture people's names and e-mail as they come to your webpage during the time of the deal. Now, you can send them your free report on "How to Pick the Best Dentist," or your video series on "The Best Ways to Avoid Cavities While Eating Sweet Foods." Think back to what we discussed earlier with regard to videos. Now, all of this can be put to use. Once again, social buying platforms are ideal ways to market your office, but now do you see how, even here, the true value of marketing is consistently adding massive value?

3. Patients who love your deal will come to you after seeing you and getting to know you online. These patients are the ones more likely to buy from you. They've read your reviews, they've watched your videos (because I know you've put them up before you do this), and they have been exposed to the culture of your office through your presence on-line. Essentially, you have created an office or presence outside of your location, and that is what you're being evaluated on. These patients are more web savvy as well. This could mean great things for you if you position your delivery intelligently. What do I mean by this? Quite simply, these patients will be more likely to write a review about your online presence, driving even more referrals to you.

4. Patients have pre-paid for your specific featured deal. Isn't that what we as dentists all try to endorse? This almost guarantees that they will come into your office and at least get some form of treatment done. In our practice, the concept of *prepay* is very prevalent since it eliminates so much unnecessary work.

After reading all of this, I'm sure you're thinking, *Okay, how can I sign up and make this work for my office?* Well, not so fast! You've got to have a few things in order before launching your intent for new patients.

FIVE ABSOLUTELY NECESSARY ELEMENTS YOU MUST HAVE BEFORE RUNNING A FEATURE WITH GROUPON.COM OR ANY OTHER SOCIAL MARKETING SITE.

1. **Set up your Online Presence Triangle.** There is no point in screaming to the world who you are if you don't have your online structure set up to serve your patients effectively with your business. Aside from this, you will end up shooting yourself in the foot if thousands of people come to your website and it is poorly designed or does not give them immediate value. Set up this triangle for your practice, make sure you can capture e-mail addresses, have a YouTube channel, have videos on your website, and have a presence on Facebook. Unlike a print piece where you may have your website address listed at the bottom, with your Groupon feature all of those details are just *one click* of the mouse away. Prospective patients can easily check out your entire online presence within seconds and make buying decisions on whether to come into your office for your featured deal.

2. **Design a website** that has a framework integrating the top five things your website should do for your patients. Please re-read this section as it is so important when you run your feature. I have seen great deals from other dentists flop because their website was set up so poorly. With a stronger online presence, you can also command a higher price on your deal since people will immediately see the value of your brand online. Get your website dialed in for success. Do it *now*!

3. **Let your patients schedule appointments online.** Yes, I know this is a part of an effective website setup, but it's also important for Groupon patients; this demographic of patients is used to making buying decisions online, so give them a way to schedule their appointments online as well. In your appointment request form on your website, have a dropdown menu item for Groupon patients. I emphasize this because, just as we talked about earlier, it's important to know how you're at-

tracting your patients so that you can plan their treatments effectively and have them return.

4. **Present a reasonable number of stellar reviews.** People will read only a few reviews at most about your practice, but they like to see that others have reviewed you as well. My advice is to run your Groupon after you have some reviews in the mix that give your prospective patients something to smile about. You're more likely to get purchases this way rather than throwing out an offer when you have no reviews.

5. **Train your front office team** on how Groupon works and how to talk to those patients coming in who bought a Groupon. This includes organizing the deal vouchers and marking them as redeemed when patients come in with their printed vouchers. Your staff should express excitement that patients purchased something online. The cheer in their voice alone will make patients excited that they bought your deal.

Having all of these online elements successfully in place will greatly contribute to your success when you run an online promotion. What happens after those patients come in, get services, and then leave your office? Well, aside from the tips you are learning from what we've laid out here, what is something specific you can do for these patients? In this case, let's say patients came in through the Groupon promotion. You would first collect their e-mail addresses that you should have captured on your dental management software as they came to your office. Second, e-mail them saying that you made a short *thank you* video for them. In the video, explain how you are grateful for them having found your office through Groupon (or any other promotion), and you would love for them to consider you for their future dental care. In your video, you can express that because they came to your office through this promotion, your office is offering them 10 percent off their next visit. Make it easy for them to come in by placing one button under the video that says *Make an appointment*, which gives them the option to take action immediately. You can host this video on YouTube on a webpage of your website. The overall framework would be just one page on your website, with one *Make an appointment* button under the video. Tell your webmaster to make this page an unmarked page on your site so that your regular visitors will not be able to look up the page—only the people you send that specific link to.

The goal here is simple. You acknowledged and thanked them for coming, and then you offered them something else for returning. Also keep in mind that you can change things up. Rather than 10 percent off, you can offer complimentary whitening trays, movie tickets, or even a specific discount on cosmetic dental services. The important thing is to acknowledge, thank, and reach out. In doing so, you will enhance your relationship you have with your patients as well. What's nice about doing this online is that once it is done, you can easily send it out again for any other online promotion you.

VIDEO

If you are looking for content on video, re-read the video chapter. I really encourage you to harness the power of the video medium for marketing your office. An easy place to start is the Frequently Asked Questions (FAQs). Get a camera and start shooting the FAQ section, and now you have some content that you can place up on your website. Don't be like every other dental office website; be unique in your creativity and utilize this edge you now have because of your new knowledge about videos.

15 CALLS A DAY STRATEGY

This is what I use to get our front office staff to consistently make calls and get patients back in. You will see that, if done correctly and collectively, it is a very powerful strategy that maximizes your office staff's efforts and encourages patients to return.

I started by giving my staff an overview of the ATR mind-set and the value of patients' returns. After they agreed that having patients return is an effective way of growing the practice, I then used the logic of numbers to illustrate the advantage of everyone working together to get patients back into the office.

I encourage you to copy and use this strategy below. We have made thousands of dollars getting our patients back to us through the use of e-mails and phone calls.

Below is a copy of what I gave my front office team on the day of the meeting, starting with the priority checklist and ending at the section titled three most important areas to focus your energy on during the workday:

PRIORITY CHECKLIST FOR YOUR DAILY PERFORMANCE GOALS

THE 3 MOST IMPORTANT ASPECTS OF GROWING YOUR OFFICE.

1. Attract new patients.
2. Create effective treatment plans for the patients who come in.
3. Return patients in a *timely and consistent* manner.

Basically this is the ATR formula. You need all three in order to have a successful formula. But also realize that they are not equal portions. The *return* aspect is the most influential portion in growing your office. Why?

1. Not everyone will do all of the work you recommend in the treatment plan that day. Therefore, even if they do some of the work, you still need to have them return for the other part. If you do not employ an effective follow-up system, your patients will not return.
2. The more a patient returns to your office, the more exposure he gets to your team, the dentists, and your customer-service environment. This means he or she is more likely to refer others as well.

3. Many people will come in, get the treatment plan, and then expect you to hold their hand through the process. If you don't call them back in, you have already failed without even realizing it.

Make at least fifteen phone calls for the day to patients who have already been in the office.

1. Schedule these patients back into the office on the first phone call. If they schedule, no e-mail is necessary.
2. If you speak to them and they do not schedule, post-date a follow-up e-mail and a phone call to get them back into the office. Even if they say they are not ready right now, you must still post-date an e-mail to approach them again at a later date.
3. If you call and you leave a voice-mail, you must also send an e-mail referencing your voice-mail and ask them to return.
4. If they request that you do not call them back, then do not call or e-mail them again.

Everyone is required to call at least fifteen people and everyone is required to schedule at least two or three people for that day from calls that they made. So, if a new patient calls and makes an appointment, it does not count toward your required two or three appointments.

HERE IS THE FORMULA:

4 people making 15 calls a day
=60 calls
4 people calling x 2 appointments scheduled per person calling
= 8 appointments scheduled every day
8 x 5 workdays
= 40 more people on the schedule every week!!!!!

This is all due to a *collective* effort where it's a priority to schedule appointments.

THREE MOST IMPORTANT AREAS TO FOCUS YOUR ENERGY ON DURING THE WORKDAY:

1. **Making phone calls** to get patients back into the office using the Formula Outlined.
2. **Planning new patients' treatments** effectively and being prepared for the requirements of their insurance prior to their arrival or during their treatment plan. This includes filling out the insurance benefits form to know what is and isn't covered and knowing what procedures are downgraded.
3. **Billing** out procedures for every patient. Our goal is to bill for all procedures the day that we do them.

REFERRAL PROGRAM (OR ACKNOWLEDGMENT PROGRAM)

Looking at practice growth from the framework of an ATR mind-set is an effective way to evaluate the flow of patients that come through your office. All three stages will help you attract even more patients through the power of referrals. In fact, when I started evaluating where our best patients came from, it was, without a doubt, through internal referrals from existing patients who had gotten treatment themselves and then returned. In other words, they had gone through the three stages of ATR. They had a complete experience, from finding out about us to receiving treatment from us. These were the patients that referred others, and those they referred already had the confidence of trust and transparency built into their mind-set. When I evaluated the financial impact this had on the practice, it was obvious that these patients that came from other patients of ours usually *spent more money in the office, had a greater sense of appreciation, and were more likely to keep coming back to us.* With this in mind, we started to reward those patients that referred their friends and family to us.

There are two ways to give thanks to patients who have referred someone to you. The first way is to send them something. This can include baked goods from a local bakery, movie tickets, or free Zoom teeth whitening. When you do, send a *handwritten* message saying thank you for supporting your office and entrusting you with their precious family and friends. Tell them you appreciate that they are helping you grow your practice. This is a wonderful way to reward your patients. Most successful dental practices have, at one time or another, been involved in rewarding their patients with gifts such as the ones I've mentioned. Simple gifts are all you really need here. Even a pair of movie tickets goes a long way since it shows patients you care and you appreciate that they sent someone your way. *Never let a referral go unacknowledged. Acknowledgment is key!*

The second one really creates a buzz and will create tremendous interactivity within your *entire* patient-base. **Start an online promotion or contest** to offer a sizable prize to the patient that refers the most patients in the next two to four months. Here are the steps you need to put this into action:

1. Send all of your patients an e-mail saying that you are starting a contest giveaway for the patient who refers the most patients to your office in four months. In the e-mail send them a link to a video that you, their dentist, shot for them explaining the contest. Remember----> E-mail with a link---> goes to your Facebook page that has the video on it---> where people comment on the promotion.

2. In the video, tell them that the first patient to refer at least ten of their friends or family will win a sizable gift certificate or $1,000 in cash paid directly to them. Let them know that you will be announcing the winner on Facebook. If you get ten new patients who actually need some treatment, the return on your investment will be worth the money spent.

CONTEST RULES

1. To win, you must refer at least ten new patients to the office who actually need dental treatment. Due to the nature of this contest and the

high-value prizes awarded to the winners, you must refer patients who need more than just a cleaning.

2. You must be a fan of our Facebook page, and so must the person you refer.
3. In the event that more than one referring patient qualifies for the prize, then the first-prize winner will be selected at random.
4. The top three referring patients will get a prize with the first place winner getting the main prize and the rest getting other prizes, such as gift certificates to Amazon with different dollar amounts.

There are quite a few benefits that come from running a contest like this. First, you raise brand awareness for your practice. Second, most patients have never seen a dental office run something like this online, so you appear to be forward thinking. Your patient-base will start interacting more on your Facebook page and also tell their friends about it. Third, you will get more new patients to your office and also build your patient-base on Facebook as well.

REPORTS YOU MUST RUN EVERY MONTH

Unscheduled treatment plans: I can't say enough about the importance of this report. It gives you immediate feedback on all of the patients with treatment plans. It's for patients who have not gotten it done and have no appointment to return and complete treatment. Look at this report when you need to know who needs to return. If the schedule looks light, this is the report I pull. My team starts calling to schedule these patients. Have your staff go through each patient who needs treatment, assess their specific situation, and call them up with a plan of action. Another approach is to actually have the dentist e-mail that person who needs a significant amount of treatment. The dentist offers to help and reminds the patients that taking care of their teeth is something that will be rewarding as the years go by. Then, after you e-mail them, a few days later have your staff follow that up with a phone call. Patients will feel as if their treatment is really important and that you do really care that it gets done. Remember, following up is important since patients often need us to hold their hand to get them back into the office, while encouraging them to get treatment done.

Follow-up report: In our offices, we call this the office journal. We use Dentrix, and the office journal is a detailed call-back log of all the patients you need to contact because they didn't schedule an appointment before they left your office. This is more specific than the unscheduled treatment plan report since it targets those patients your staff made specific notes on to call back. You need to have this. For instance, if you saw a patient and she told you she needed to speak to her husband, dad, mom or someone else before she starts treatment, you should make a post-dated note of this. Then, on that specific date, somewhere in the future, you should follow up with her by calling and asking if she had a chance to speak with that person. Your front office team could say, "I was looking over your x-rays with Dr. SuperDentist, and he mentioned that the upper right side really should be done soon because he saw some decay under that crown. Did you get a chance to speak to your husband about getting your treatment done? We have an appointment available for you next week in the morning. What's a good time for you?"

Printing out a monthly follow-up report keeps you in touch with the patients you should call back. Think of it in terms of attraction, treatment planning, and returning. If you don't have a return plan for them, you are missing out on the most effective way for you to grow your office. This report enables you to re-engage with those patients who need to come back but do not have an appointment. The office journal report gives your specific, personalized descriptions of your patients, which you can use to connect with them to guide them back into the office.

Insurance aging report: This is a great report that gives you feedback on the pending claims you've sent out that have not returned with a payment. You should be looking at this and having your staff follow up with denied claims and those that have taken over thirty days to pay out. Always aim to keep accounts receivables very low. Following up here with the insurance companies will help you do that.

New patient report: You should know exactly how many new patients are coming to your office every month and where they're coming from. When I say *where*, I mean where they originated from. Was it another patient, insurance, or a marketing campaign? Knowing this information will allow you to market and target those areas more heavily. Even if they came through their insurance, realize that they likely looked you up online and that having an effective Online Presence Triangle is important for being selected!

DENTAL INSURANCE

I did not include dental insurance in this book because it is such a large topic in dentistry. There are too many opinions, most of them emotionally charged with some facet of frustration because of what is happening with insurance and dentistry. Insurance companies want to pay out for the least costly procedures and be guarded against covering many advanced procedures in dentistry today. The insurance line can sometimes also be a gray patch of undefined answers. You must have a philosophy that can guide you thorough these patches of confusion. Some dentists hate insurances, while others don't mind, and then others love them. Here is where I stand.

When someone goes to work at Apple, IBM, or any big company with thousands of employees, they get health benefits. Some of those benefits include dental as well. Most people getting these insurances are not aware of their dental benefits and what kind of treatment is covered. They simply have insurance. It doesn't make any sense to miss out on attracting those people since they are great prospective patients who have the disposable income to pay for dentistry. The detail of what is covered and what is not covered is what we dentists focus on, while the patient only knows that insurance covers cleanings two times a year and a percentage of some dental treatment. You can't expect patients to know much more than that.

Here is how you can make dental insurance work for you: Don't categorize that patient as an HMO or PPO patient and view them with those treatment filters. All patients, for the most part, want high-standard treatment, so treatment plan accordingly.

Remember the real meaning of marketing is to consistently add massive value to your patients. If you are doing this, your patients will know because they all want value, not what is just covered by their insurance. If you show them and *educate* them on what they actually need, what the best treatment is for them, and then financially give them a way to get that treatment started, they will be more likely to pay for services that are considered elective by their insurance. In my offices, I take all insurances, except for a few really outrageous HMO plans that are just another form of legalized fraud. For the most part, we even take most HMOs and almost all PPO plans. I have gotten some wonderful patients through our insurance plans. I never identify my patients' potential in doing the best quality of treatment based on the type of insurance they have. Treating them with respect and giving them the best treatment, most of the time, is far beyond what is actually covered in their plan so they do have to pay out of pocket. Usually, they don't have a problem with it. Remember, when your patients trust you and know you have their best interest in mind, they will pay for your services. Also, remember that when they walk into your office and it's a world-class design indicating that you are not the average discount store, they raise their financial capacity to pay as well. Most of the time it's not a money issue; it's usually that they haven't linked enough value to your suggested treatment. Using what you have learned in this book about attracting, treatment planning, and having them return to your office, you can condition them to see your office and team beyond what they have been thinking. Let them see you as different. Re-invent dentistry in their minds as well and you'll see that no matter what insurance anyone has, they too will gravitate to a higher value and better treatment. Most of the time.

Another benefit in taking most insurance plans is the referral factor. All of those patients with insurance may have friends with no dental insurance, and you can now get them in as patients too through your referral program.

FOLLOW UP AUTO-PILOT WITH DEMANDFORCE

What you're about to read will absolutely blow your mind and get you even more excited about putting it all together. I wish this technology existed ten years ago so that I could have started out fresh from the start. We have emphasized the importance of having a mind-set that supports our system to attract, treatment plan, and return our patients. Mastering our Online Presence Triangle shows us how to put it all together so we position our online influence intelligently and strategically. But how do you execute all of this? Is there a technology or tool that puts it all together? Enter Demandforce.

Demandforce is nothing short of awesome! It has made it easier and *automatic* for me to execute many of the strategies that this book teaches. Let me be clear; I am not sponsored by them. I simply love their technology. It's automatic, which means no effort is required on my part when initiating the system.

The first thing you will need from your patients is their e-mail address; it is the cornerstone of the Online Presence Triangle. Second, put their cell phone number in their chart. Mobile phone numbers are the norm these days, so I am sure it's obvious why. Here is how it works and what it means for your practice.

Demandforce extracts your patients' e-mail addresses and integrates them into their content management software specifically designed for dental practices. *This portal and system is your practice's dashboard for managing patient appointments, follow up and integration, recall visits, promotional and social media campaigns, online reviews, specific revenue generated, and even newsletters.* Let's structure our review into points of influence starting with online reviews, appointment follow up, and campaigns and newsletters.

Online reviews: When patients leave your office they get an e-mail asking them to rate or review their visit. Your patients write reviews on you and your office, and those reviews are then directly shot out to Google. Here is where the magic really happens as Google uses these exact reviews to post onto your Google Places page. The software goes another step forward when it gives your patients an option to refer a friend to your office through a button in their e-mail that says *Refer a Friend*. If your patients are giving you great reviews, it only makes sense they'll click the button and refer someone else. This is all done automatically. Let's not forget the more *social proof* you have through your reviews, the more optimized your practice gets on Google search engines, and the more validation you give to patients searching for a potential dentist or learning more about your services. *Note*- recently Google made some changes as to the placement of third-party reviews. Specifically, Demandforce reviews still maintained their relevancy, but their positioning on the Google Places page has changed.

Appointments and follow up: If your patients have an appointment with you sometime in the future, the Demandforce system will automatically e-mail them, text them, and remind them of their appointment a few days prior. On the reminder, your patients will have the option to confirm their appointment or reschedule it. If they reschedule, your staff gets notified and confirms the new appointment date. All this is *automatically* done without your having to send out e-mails. The timelines can be set to your preferences. For instance, you can remind patients of their appointment two days before or two hours before using a text message, e-mail, or both. The technology is mobile phone capable so if your patients prefer the texting/SMS medium of communication, you can bypass the e-mail communication and use text messages only. This eliminates your staff from having to call and confirm appointments since all of the appointment confirmations can be seen on your online dashboard. This function alone has allowed our front office staff to focus on more important revenue-generating tasks.

Campaigns and newsletters: You can immediately generate revenue with a single online campaign. I have generated over $30,000 with some campaigns that I continue to do every year. Since Demandforce captures all of your patients' e-mail addresses, you can have total access to sending them an e-mail that alerts them to come into your office because of your current promotion. Let's not forget that marketing equals consistently adding massive value. For example, send your patients an e-mail through your Demandforce dashboard indicating you made a special video for them on teeth whitening. In the e-mail, provide a link for them to make an appointment, refer a friend, or even become a fan on Facebook. You've done two things here: you've educated them on teeth whitening, and you've given them an opportunity to make an appointment through your e-mail system via Demandforce. The new world order in marketing our practice demands that we give first, and then receive. When you send your patients an informational piece or link using Demandforce and then give them the option to schedule an appointment automatically, it dramatically increases appointments made.

Complete tracking of revenue generated: When your patients make appointments through your promotions and campaigns, Demandforce extracts the data from their patient ledgers and documents how much money they actually spent at your office because they came in after an e-mail campaign you sent out through the Demandforce dashboard. This is valuable because you can see how much revenue was generated for every visit along with how many and which patients came into your office due to an e-mail promotion.

Demandforce is a powerful tool and system that works while you sleep. Our front office team uses it daily and loves how easily it has been integrated into their daily routine. Once again, it is not a substitute for your online presence, nor will it create one if you are not already set up. Your entire online presence should flow when you initiate the tactical guidelines of your Online Presence Triangle. You still need to have your website that gets prospective patient e-mails in exchange for a value-added piece of content. Keep an appointment page on your website for all those who simply visit your site. Your practice website will always be critical to your online presence. *Demandforce can help you take your entire online presence and amplify its impact via strategic campaigns, follow up, appointment recalls, online reviews, and an organized patient e-mail database.*

Next, I will review 15 strategy points when using Demandforce. If you already use Demandforce in your practice then follow along in your Demandforce dashboard, if not, I would suggest integrating it into your practice. Some of the content here is very similar in theme and wording to some earlier sections of the book, but I have specifically applied it to the use of Demandforce. There has never been a better way to keep your patients engaged and grow your practice through the use of *automated* technology tools.

TOP 15 WAYS TO USE DEMANDFORCE TO SKYROCKET YOUR REVENUE

1. MAKE SURE YOU GET EVERYONE'S E-MAIL ADDRESS

This is the cornerstone of the Demandforce technology! It sounds really simple, but some practices make it more complicated than it has to be. You have to change the mentality of your front office team from thinking they have to send out postcards, phone call reminders, and letters in the mail to have patients return to the office. Think of Demandforce as a new and much more effective *system* for running your office. Tell your staff that your goal is to communicate with your patients online, and their e-mail is even more important than getting their home address! A lot of office managers and treatment coordinators ask for e-mail by saying that they want a patient's e-mail to "send" them special promotions and offers! That's horrible! **No one wants another "special offer" from your office! What your patients really want is informative content driven places that they can go to that helps THEM!** Isn't that what the entire online world really is? Content in some form or another that is useful for specific people. That is what you have to give them!

To easily capture their e-mail address: Here are <u>4 Key Points</u> to go over with your patients without them feeling weird about it.

Tell them that you need to make sure they are in your automated system so that you never *forget about their recall cleaning visits,* and this way a reminder will go out to them every 3 or 6 months informing them of their cleanings. Tell them that you won't be sending a ton of e-mails and just specific ones for their appointments only.

You need it so it is possible for them to make their appointments online, get a reminder of an appointment, and confirm their appointment without them having to call the office. Patients love this type of convenience so show them that your office has the technology to give them more *convenient* means of communication.

ALWAYS suggest that a patient schedule their next appointment before leaving your front office EVEN IF its 6 months from now. This eliminates the wasted effort spent trying to get them back in for their recall via outdated and traditional methods. When you make these suggestions you must also do this ONE THING. *Tell them they can <u>reschedule their appointment online</u> through a click of a button if they need to.* This way there is no feeling of being boxed into a commitment 6 months prior to an appointment time. Look at this like a *risk eliminator* so they actually take the initiative and schedule the appointment. You'll see that when they get an appointment reminder online they usually make it to that appointment.

Lastly let them know that your office has specials exclusive to just your online patient *system.* This is important, let them know it is a system. Don't just say that they will get an e-mail from you! Demandforce is an *automatic* system that makes it easier for your patients to return to your office with less effort and time spent on painstaking administrative tasks.

2. SEND OUT CAMPAIGNS

This is such an effective and immediate revenue generator! Now that you have all of their e-mail addresses, all you have to do is send out regular campaigns to have them come back to your office. You don't want to slam them with a barrage of specials and campaigns every week, but you should effectively send out three or four big campaigns every year. You can do more, but you should always know your patients and gauge how much communication they want from you.

As soon as you send out a campaign, you can see how many people have come in due to that specific e-mail you sent them and how much revenue was generated from that specific campaign. This is powerful information! A campaign every dentist should be participating in is the "End of the Year Use your Insurance Benefits Campaign," which goes out to all of your patients. In this e-mail, just let them know that their insurance benefits will expire at the end of the year and if they need any treatments, this would be a great time to get it done. *Note: Even if they do not have insurance it's okay; send this e-mail to them anyway so that they can see what you do for your insured patients as they may ask you if you can work out some arrangement for them since they are paying cash.* This one always generates massive revenue in our office. Here is the copy that I wrote up that created over $20,000 in revenue from patients and insurance combined. Not a bad way to boost your end-of-the-year collections! This also generated over fifty visits in our office! Best of all, I didn't have to pay anything to run this since the Demandforce system did the whole thing for me.

YEAR END INSURANCE REMINDER

WOW! I can't believe we are approaching the end of the year already! I can remember when we JUST began THIS YEAR. We just wanted to email out a quick reminder to take advantage of your Dental Insurance benefits before the end of the year. Insurance benefits expire at the year end. Request an appointment online or call our office to schedule an appointment before the end of the year to take advantage of your insurance benefits.
Offer expires 5/20/2011
Some restrictions apply

Request Appointment

Year End Insurance Reminder using Demandforce

You can send out all different types of campaigns. You can use templates for different treatment types if you would rather not write it. There are some excellent templates available for Zoom whitening, Invisalign, and smile makeovers. All of these can be found within the Demandforce dashboard for your office under the campaigns section.

3. SET UP YOUR BLOG

Having a blog linked to your website is one of the most effective ways you can share content with your patients. Think of the blog like a platform that holds all of your content. All of your articles, videos, and interesting points of communication should all be kept on your blog. All of the content that you place on the blog should have a comments section as well. You should also have one button on your blog so that patients can instantly set up appointments. The question you should ask yourself is what kind of people should regularly visit your blog and how? The answer is *Everyone* and through *Demandforce*. Everyone who is a patient should be exposed to your blog, and you can easily do that with Demandforce. This brings us to the monthly newsletter.

4. CREATE A MONTHLY NEWSLETTER

Newsletters are very effective, especially when they direct patients to your blog. Go to Demandforce, click on *campaign* and then *create newsletter*. Over here you'll find templates to use as well. I like writing my own, so I can suggest that our patients go to our blog and place that link in the text. Let's say you posted a cool article that you had written for your blog. You'd mention it in your newsletter and then instruct them to go to your blog to check it out. Once again, this drives traffic back to your website and blog, and eventually your office. Here is the great exception: some patients may not even go to your blog; rather, they will immediately make an appointment off your Demandforce e-mail when they see it! Do you see how once again, we are giving your patients multiple ways to get into your office!

5. SEND OUT VIDEO LINKS TO YOUR PATIENTS

Videos have an extremely high-perceived value, so this means that if you tell your patients you shot a video for them, they are more likely to go where you direct them to view it. You must make it a goal to shoot some informative videos and place them on YouTube, your blog, and Facebook. Now, you can use the newsletter feature in Demandforce to send them a link to your YouTube page or even your blog. *Note: Facebook is an important platform for your video as well.*

6. RE-SEND OPT-INS

When existing patients come into your office, ask them if they got an e-mail confirming their appointment and tell them about this *cool and unique feature* that your office has to make it convenient for them to make and confirm appointments *online*. If they tell you that they didn't receive any e-mails from you, look at the dashboard and re-send their opt-in e-mail. Here's how:

Go to Demandforce, click on the *appointments* tab, and then scroll down. You will see a box that says *Offline Appointments*. This is an important feature to check daily since you might have a patient that simply forgot to opt-in to getting e-mail and text communications from your office. Sometimes when you miss an e-mail it gets backlogged and moves all the way down your list, and you forgot that it was ever in your inbox. Demandforce has a solution for this: re-send the opt-in e-mail! Simply put, send them another e-mail asking if they want to be a part of your *online community*. This can be easily done in the *Offline Appointments* box by clicking on *Resend opt-in*.

7. BEFORE PATIENTS LEAVE YOUR OFFICE, SCHEDULE THEM FOR AN APPOINTMENT.

This is huge, and so many offices miss the mark here. Make it easy on yourself and your staff. The rule is to have patients schedule their next appointment for a cleaning, recall, or treatment before they leave your office, even if they don't know their schedule for sure. Why? Because with Demandforce, the system will send them an e-mail indicating their appointment time. At this point, they have the option of rescheduling the appointment. The key here is that they are in the loop of your Demandforce system, and if they have to reschedule, Demandforce will have them choose another time to come in. The bottom line is that they are in your system, so no one forgets to call them, e-mail them, or any other excuse that you can think of. I even have my staff do this with patients' six-month cleaning appointments. When they leave our office, we will skip forward on our Dentrix appointment book and put them in six months from the current date. We have our Demandforce preferences set up so that the software shoots them an e-mail two weeks prior to their appointment date and another one three days prior. Patients love this! If they really need to, they can reschedule at any one of these two points, but they rarely do this. This eliminates the cost of having your staff use their time getting patients back in, sending out postcard reminders, and using phone time. *Best of all, it's all automatic!*

8. TALK TO THE PATIENT, AND ASK THEM ABOUT THE DF SYSTEM.

Get your team excited about this system and have them endorse it to your patients. Whenever someone in your office shows passion or excitement about new technology, it creates a desire in the patient to be a part of the system. This way, more patients will give you their e-mail addresses, and more of them will opt-in to actually use the system. When you, the dentist, talk about this new way of communicating with your patients, it raises your perceived value as a *high-tech* dentist. You also learn from the patients what they really like about the system so that you can replicate those positive experiences.

9. SET UP YOUR BIRTHDAY GREETINGS

Go to Demandforce, find the *Setup* link in the upper right-hand corner of the page, and click on *Birthday* under the communications pane. Make sure you have your system set up so that patients get a birthday e-mail from you. In this e-mail, you can give them something for their birthday, such as a free cleaning or a special deal on a dental treatment they might need. Even if you don't give away something, it's okay because your patient will still appreciate being *acknowledged by you on their birthday.*

10. USE HOTLIST

You will always have a group of patients ready to come in if you have a sudden cancellation. These are the patients you want to add in your Hotlist section. On the dashboard under the Confirmations box on the right-hand side of your screen are all your confirmations for the next seven days. If someone doesn't confirm an appointment and you want to fill his or her spot, you can access your Hotlist and contact one of those patients for a last-minute appointment.

11. SET UP YOUR FACEBOOK PAGE AND INTEGRATE IT WITH FACEBOOK CONNECT

You've got to have your Facebook page set up. With around 800 million people on Facebook and with one out of nine people on the planet with a Facebook account, you need to be connected and willing to go where your patients are spending their time. An estimated 700 billion minutes a month are spent on Facebook. If you don't have your Facebook page set up, stop reading this and go do it now! Your Facebook page is another area to post content and send patients.

The Facebook Connect feature lets you market your Facebook page and also informs your patients that they can get appointments through your page. You can use Demandforce to send your patients a newsletter indicating that you posted a video or a link to an article (which can go to your blog) on your Facebook page. Not only will you get more fans from the pool of patients in your office but, even more important, you will be providing some great content, all hosted on your Facebook page. While your fans or patients are on your page, they can also click on the appointment tab and make an appointment. This will take them directly to your office from your Facebook page. *Demandforce's Facebook Connect feature gives your patients yet another way to get into your office.*

12. USE THE DIGITAL CONSULTANT FOR PRACTICE FEEDBACK AND TEAM MEETINGS

One of the most important things to evaluate in your business should always be consumer feedback and how that feedback compares to others in your industry. Go to Demandforce and click on the *Digital Consultant* tab. This tab shows you how your office has been rated by your patients' experience through the course of your selected time frame. You can now use this data *in your office meetings* to improve areas of weakness while duplicating strengths.

13. MAKE CONSISTENT USE OF TIMELY BY DEMANDFORCE

This is another very effective feature to help automate your Facebook and Twitter presence. As a Demandforce user you can utilize Timely directly from your Demandforce dashboard. The Timely feature enables you to post status updates or content directly to your Facebook and Twitter pages *automatically at a pre-selected schedule* of your choice. For instance, you could set up weeks and weeks of Facebook posts and Timely will post them to your pages automatically at the most reader friendly time for your audience. In addition, the feature will also track your posts and give you feedback on which posts got the most comments and reach within your audience. This is great for saving time and outsourcing some of the social media duties to a reliable front office team member. The best thing, you or a staff member can do this all from within the Demandforce dashboard.

14. INVITE YOUR PATIENTS TO "LIKE" YOU ON FACEBOOK

This is something that every dentist using Demandforce should be doing. Go to campaigns--->Custom promotions--->Create Newsletter and, under Reputation Builder, select the tab that says, "Are you on Facebook? So are we!" This will pop up a standard template Facebook invitation letter. I suggest you tweak it according to your office events and, in the message, tell patients you have *posted a video* on your Facebook page and, if they like, please click the "Like" button. Essentially, you are asking them to do something for you but, before they do, you are giving them some valuable content on your site. This is a great way to launch your fan-base on Facebook.

15. SET YOUR REVIEW FEATURE PREFERENCE TO ONE WEEK.

Demandforce has an automatic review request feature. This is cool! The Demandforce system will automatically send your patients an online review to fill out at the preset time of your choice. I suggest you send this out for one week. It's not too long for them to forget about you, but long enough for most types of post-op pain situations to get better. If you did some dental treatment on someone the day before you ask them to review you and your office, and they are still in pain, they'll be more likely to write you a less than stellar review. Make sure you ask your patients to write reviews when they are in a peak state and not in pain! One week is a reasonable amount of time for most post-op pain to dissipate.

So, there you have it! *The 15 Ways to use Demandforce to Skyrocket your Revenue.* If you follow just ten of these valuable keys, you will still see a noticeable rise in your patient-base and consistent, recurring appointments. I really encourage you to harness the power of Demandforce to help create your social media footprint and fuel your practice growth.

GREAT LINKS

There is an endless supply of information, websites, applications, and plug-ins that exist in the online universe. I wanted to give you a few of my favorite places where I collect information and continually educate myself on Internet marketing. Here are some amazing online resources will help you accomplish the goals presented in this book:

http://www.drganatra.com

This is my very own blog for dentists about *Dentistry, Lifestyle, and Marketing*. All of these are passions of mine...check out some insightful perspectives that you can use in Life and Dentistry. Check it out and let me know what you think!

http://www.dentalpracticemastery.com

My free online 3 part video training series on how to Build, Market, and Grow your practice. This is truly the best place to join me personally and keep learning at higher levels.

http://www.evernote.com

One of my favorite tools online. This will make it possible for you to live a paperless lifestyle without having multiple windows open on your computer. You can screen-capture any web page and come back to it later, write notes, and create folders and files to organize your content. You can do all of this through your phone as well and have it automatically sync to your desktop. Love this one. Oh, and it's also free!

http://www.socialmediaexaminer.com

Latest news and know-hows of social media. Here you'll find many interesting articles, tips, and tricks to help you put it all together online.

http://www.emarketingvids.com

Tips and tricks for online videos, Facebook, and Twitter. I've met the founders of this site, and they are all sincerely passionate about social media and spreading the good word.

http://www.odesk.com

Outsource anything, evaluate bids on projects you outsource, monitor work history, hire, and pay at a competitive rate. This is an amazing tool. I currently use Odesk for many of my own projects. You can contract work out to different countries around the world and have it completed while you sleep! There truly is some great talent here. The next time you need an online graphic or even a print piece done for your office, post a job on Odesk.com and hire the best. The platform give you a chance to view potential online employees' work history and ratings. Spend some time here and pick some talent!

http://www.elance.com

Similar to oDesk with minor differences.

http://guru.com

Similar to Elance and oDesk. Check them all out and see for yourself which one you prefer.

http://www.99designs.com

Crowdsourcing is powerful. This site enables you to have a "crowd" or a large amount of people bid on your jobs. For instance, if you need a logo for your practice then submit it to 99 Designs and have tens to hundreds of people give you logo designs for it. You only pay when you pick one. Great resource!

http://www.helpareporter.com

Get publicity and media coverage from reporters who need information that you may have. If you want to get your name out there then check this site out. A local writer or T.V. reporter may need the expert help of a dentist. This resource is the perfect tool to get you started in building your expert status. Explore it!

www.trafficgeyser.com

The best online tool for getting your videos out to the public, creating backlinks, and establishing dominance through a viral presence online. You can shoot videos, post articles, podcasts, and blog posts to multiple sites, all with the touch of one button! I love this software and couldn't speak more highly of it.

www.tubetoolbox.com-

I mentioned this in the YouTube section. It's simple to use, it works for building a following on YouTube, and it's cheap at only $10 a month.

www.wildfire.com

Great for creating contests that drive fans to your Facebook page. Get your web designer to help you utilize wildfire.

www.contestburner.com

An online tool for creating viral contests for your online community. Another resource worth exploring.

www.basecamphq.com

Project management software. If you have a large project and need to delegate tasks to those around you or to those around the world, this is a great way to keep track of it all.

www.mindmeister.com

An excellent way to collect your thoughts about any sort of creative process in your practice or life. It's like having a whiteboard to write out processes, connect thoughts, and organize a project so that you can see how everything in your practice, or project, comes together.

www.involver.com

Makes it possible to customize your social media platform and integrate elements of coupons, contests, landing pages, and other resources into your Facebook page. A wonderful resource that allows you to pull your YouTube channel into your Facebook page.

Made in the USA
Lexington, KY
29 June 2013